T0361148

The Nylon Spinners

First published in 1971 *The Nylon Spinners* presents one of the few detailed and firsthand studies of the impact of productivity bargaining on the shop floor and makes an important contribution to the social and psychological understanding of human behaviour. Productivity bargaining has moved far beyond its earlier preoccupation with the wage-effort bargain. It is becoming increasingly apparent that it may have profound direct effects on the attitudes and expertise of managers, on the institutions and climate of industrial relations, and on the motivations and satisfactions of operatives. The problems of industrial relations are not the primary focus of this study. But the growing recognition of the gap between the formal and informal systems on the shop floor, and of the limitations of managerial control, emphasizes the importance of a deeper understanding of industrial behaviour. What motivates men not simply to go to work but to work to the best of their ability?

This book is essential for students of the behavioral sciences, industrial relations, labour economics and economics in general.

The Nylon Spinners

A case study in productivity bargaining and job enlargement

Stephen Cotgrove, Jack Dunham, Clive Vamplew

First published in 1971
by George Allen & Unwin Ltd.

This edition first published in 2023 by Routledge
4 Park Square, Milton Park, Abingdon, Oxon, OX14 4RN

and by Routledge
605 Third Avenue, New York, NY 10017

Routledge is an imprint of the Taylor & Francis Group, an informa business

© George Allen & Unwin Ltd., 1971

Publisher's Note
The publisher has gone to great lengths to ensure the quality of this reprint but points out that some imperfections in the original copies may be apparent.

Disclaimer
The publisher has made every effort to trace copyright holders and welcomes correspondence from those they have been unable to contact.

A Library of Congress record exists under ISBN: 0041580044

ISBN: 978-1-032-58182-8 (hbk)
ISBN: 978-1-003-44894-5 (ebk)
ISBN: 978-1-032-58183-5 (pbk)

Book DOI 10.4324/9781003448945

THE NYLON SPINNERS

A case study in productivity bargaining
and job enlargement

STEPHEN COTGROVE
JACK DUNHAM
CLIVE VAMPLEW

London · George Allen & Unwin Ltd
RUSKIN HOUSE   MUSEUM STREET

First published in 1971

ISBN 0 04 158004 4

Printed in Great Britain
in 11 point Baskerville
by Unwin Brothers Limited, Woking and London

Preface

This is a report of some aspects of a successful productivity agreement. It is also an example of collaboration between social scientists in a university and industry. In the summer of 1967 Bath University was approached by ICI to ask whether we could assist them in monitoring the introduction of a productivity agreement. They wanted independent and objective observers to see what was actually happening on the shop floor and to explore how far events took the course that it was hoped and expected they would take.

The simple solution was adopted that the University would appoint a research worker and would supervise the inquiry. The research worker would report to, and be responsible to, the University. But the costs would be met in full by ICI. In practice, the arrangement worked well. The preliminary planning was completed by the spring of 1968 and a first draft of the findings presented in the autumn.

Before accepting the task, the University asked, and ICI willingly agreed, that any findings of more general interest to social scientists should be published. In the event, we believe that this report will also be of value to industry, and it is mainly for this wider audience that the present version is published. It will, we think, be of particular interest because it provides such detailed insights into reactions on the shop floor, and also because, unlike the majority of such agreements which have been concluded in process technology plants, in this one the technology had some of the features of the assembly line.

Productivity bargaining has moved far beyond its early pre-occupation with the wage-effort bargain. It is increasingly realized that it may have profound indirect effects on the attitudes and expertise of managers, on the institutions and climate of industrial relations, and on the motivations and satisfactions of operatives. Such effects may be more important than any short-term changes in payment and manning. Indeed, one of the most significant developments in thinking on industrial relations has been the growing realization of the limits of formal control over workshop behaviour. Notably, the Donovan Commission sees plant bargaining as a means of closing the gap between the formal and informal systems.

The problems of industrial relations are not the primary focus of this study. But the growing realization of the limitations of managerial control, highlights the importance of a deeper understanding of industrial behaviour. What motivates men (operatives and managers), not simply to go to work, but more importantly, to work to the best of their ability? Recent studies in the behavioural and social sciences, for example the work of Frederick Herzberg and his associates, have had considerable impact on industrial thinking. They have challenged the view that workers are by nature lazy and work-shy and have argued that what motivates men to achievement is the chance to exercise the skills and capacities which are denied in many jobs. Job enlargement and job enrichment are among the indicated remedies. It is on such questions, on the meaning of work, its rewards and satisfactions, its frustrations and deprivations, that this study is primarily focused.

After a general review of productivity bargaining and the issues which it raises in Chapter 1, we begin in Chapter 2 by exploring recent work in the social and behavioural sciences which has implications for the motivation to work. Such findings particularly influenced the thinking behind the ICI agreement, which was conceived very much as an exercise in plant democracy and as an opportunity to achieve some improvement in motivation and satisfaction through job enlargement (Chapter 3). The working environment (job context) was found to be more important than might have been expected. Noise, heat and shift-work were tolerated by many only because the pay was high. Moreover, increase in shop-floor participation had subtle but important effects on attitudes, involvement and motivation, providing an outlet for knowledge and experience which had previously lain dormant (Chapter 4). Organizational changes in supervision and job enlargement brought a marked reduction in fatigue and boredom (Chapter 5). But here, the limits on organizational change became apparent. The technology sets the limits to the skill and task-integration that is possible. The jobs remained essentially monotonous. The success of the agreement owed much to the skill and commitment of the front-line supervisors. And it was this group who experienced particular strains in adopting the new supervisory roles which the changes required (Chapter 6). Success depended too on the preliminary consultations and involvement discussions, whose impact is explored in Chapter 7.

Judged by such criteria as reductions in manning, labour turnover and operative performance, the agreement may be considered a success (Chapter 8). Finally, in Chapter 9, we attempt to take stock, draw some lessons and look ahead. The gains were limited but real. Although most went into the agreement for the money, one of the most vivid impressions with which we are left is the emergence of latent needs for self-actualization. Despite years of work with little responsibility, the majority accepted the opportunity, even welcomed it, when offered. There has, too, been a marked improvement in teamwork and communications. But this should not lead to any expectation that the attitudes towards the effort bargain will be in any way weakened. In short, improvements in shop-floor relations can co-exist with tough bargaining over pay and an equitable distribution of the 'cake'. There is little doubt that some of the gains are permanent. But to quote a spinning operative:

> 'I don't think we're ever going to come to a stage where we can sit still and say "right, well, this is it . . . we're here". There's got to be another stage.'

This is a report on a project in which many have been involved, and to whose success many have contributed. Some of this will come through as the report unfolds. It is even more difficult than usual, therefore, to acknowledge any particular indebtedness. But we would wish to place on record at the outset our appreciation of the willing co-operation of the 'nylon-spinners' on the shop floor. It is *their* insights into the human side of work which we are here recording. We hope that we have done them justice. Chapter 1 is a shortened and simplified version of three chapters prepared by W. W. Daniel for a PEP report on productivity bargaining. We are grateful to him and to PEP for allowing us to see this before publication and for permission to print the abbreviated work here. We would also like to thank both Bill Daniel and Brian Barratt for reading the entire manuscript and for their valuable comments and suggestions.

Finally, we would like to express our thanks for the constant help and comments which we received from ICI management. Any shortcomings in the report, however, remain ours.

Bath University,   S. C.
July 1970.   J. D.
                                                                                   C. V.

Contents

CONTENTS

Chapter 1

PRODUCTIVITY BARGAINING[1]

Productivity bargaining has become enshrined in government incomes policy, has been the subject of three official or semi-official reports,[2] and has been stressed in four white papers on incomes policy as a criterion for pay increases. Twenty-five per cent[3] of all employed workers received pay increases under the productivity criterion of the incomes policy in the four years ending June 1969.[4]

Productivity bargaining has aroused enthusiastic support and equally vigorous criticism. But the debate has been complicated by the evolution of the practice and process of bargaining since Fawley.[5] Some of the later and more recent agreements have gone beyond a wage-effort bargain, which aims primarily at restraining or reducing labour costs. This book is an account of one such agreement which included among its objectives changes in industrial relations and in the motivations and satisfactions of operatives. To understand the significance of this particular agreement we must first put it in perspective by both relating it to earlier agreements, and more important, by exploring some of the wider objectives beyond a wage bargain, which it set out to achieve.

[1] This is a shortened and simplified version of three chapters from a forth-coming publication by W. W. Daniel. For a more detailed discussion, see *Beyond the Wage-work Bargain*, PEP broadsheet, 519, 1970.

[2] Royal Commission on trade unions and employers' associations: *The Donovan Report* (HMSO, 1968). See especially Research paper no. 4, *Productivity Bargaining* (HMSO, 1967). *Productivity Agreements:* NBPI Reports Nos. 36 (HMSO, 1967) and 123 (1969).

[3] The definition of the productivity criterion in the incomes policy is somewhat wider than most definitions of productivity agreements—thus it is almost certainly true that many of the agreements giving increases under the productivity criterion would not qualify within most normal definitions of the term as productivity agreements—although the 25 per cent does give some measure of the influence of the concept.

[4] NBPI Report No. 123 (1969).

[5] Allan Flanders, *The Fawley Productivity Agreements* (1964).

13

Fawley and after

The distinctive features of the early agreements were first a systematic analysis of the use of manpower and human resources at least at manual worker level (throughout an organization); secondly, an analysis of the changes necessary to use manpower more effectively; thirdly, the negotiation of these changes with the trade unions in the form of a package deal in conjunction with negotiations about increases in earnings.

At its simplest then, productivity bargaining can be seen as an aspect of wage-work bargaining in which workers or their representatives accept changes in methods or patterns of working that contribute to higher productivity in return for increases in earnings or their equivalent. It would appear that such a bargain, like all bargains, would be advantageous to both parties: the workers get higher earnings, and management gets lower costs and higher productivity. But it is not as simple as it seems. Firstly, that simple idea requires new ways of thinking from management and makes massive new demands on managers and supervisors; secondly, it conceals a challenge to some long-established and cherished trade union principles; and thirdly, it represents a change in the socio-economic status of a group or groups of employees that sets up a chain reaction between rewards, roles and relationships throughout an organization. Moreover, the concept raises fundamental ideological issues about what should be the relations between employers and unions. But before we launch into an exploration of these more fundamental issues, some brief account is necessary of the objectives of Fawley and the other early agreements.[6]

In the early 1960s several major productivity deals were concluded which were in many ways very similar and had many common features. They were all major package deals struck in capital intensive, continuous process industries; oil, chemicals and steel. They sought to diminish the chronic under-employment and misuse of human resources in these industries and to raise productivity by the following distinct but interdependent means: (*a*) controlling overtime; (*b*) reducing manning; and (*c*) creating greater flexibility.

[6] For summary, see Research Paper No. 4, *op. cit.* (HMSO, 1967).

(*a*) *Reducing or Eliminating Overtime.* A persistent and growing theme in British industrial relations during the fifties and sixties has been the growth and abuse of overtime. The argument goes as follows: Overtime is and has been paid not because overtime working is required by the demands of the job but because it is required to supplement the low base-rates of workers. This has two consequences. It means that overtime is created by the under-employment of workers during normal working hours. It becomes institutionalized and persists or grows in volume regardless of the needs of the job. It also means that a substantial proportion of the workers' time (overtime) is paid at premium rates. Productivity agreements sought to reduce or do away with overtime working by raising base-rates to maintain levels of earnings at the same time as reorganizing work so that the same or a greater volume of work was completed in normal working hours. This reduced management costs, brought an out-of-control situation into its control, but maintained workers' incomes and gave them shorter working hours and more leisure.[7]

The thinking behind these changes has been a consistent theme in subsequent productivity agreements, and while it was resisted and rejected initially, it has now become an accepted part of a new orthodoxy. It was argued strongly with impressive documentation in a research paper (No. 9) published by the Donovan Commission. The Commission largely accepted the argument. Despite this, and the number of productivity agreements that have subsequently been completed, the problem still remains. Indeed, the Prices and Incomes Board has sought a special reference on overtime working.

Such views have not gone unchallenged. It is argued that in some circumstances overtime working is necessary and can *contribute* to higher productivity. What is in doubt is how general is the abuse. The PIB clearly thinks it is very widespread. Turner,[8] however, sets forth alternative and unfashionable views that in the economy generally overtime working is, *on average*, about right from a productivity view-

[7] See *The Donovan Report*, Minutes of evidence: No. 39, Esso, No. 44, Prof. D. J. Robertson, and No. 47, O'Brien, K. Nicol.
[8] H. A. Turner, 'The Royal Commission's Research Papers'; *BJIR*, Vol. VI, No. 3, Nov. 1968.

point, that the opportunity to work overtime has considerable incidental advantages for workers, allowing them to choose between more work and more leisure as they wish and furnishing a discretionary component in their earnings that they value. Furthermore, overtime working is particularly valuable to both management and workers in industries liable to short-term fluctuations in demand which can be dealt with by variations in hours rather than by alternate dismissals and engagements.

(b) *Reduction in Manning.* Largely as a result of international comparisons, a conclusive case was made that British industry in general, and these industries in particular, were heavily overmanned. Esso, Fawley, found itself at the bottom of the Standard Oil international league. Bill Allen, an American management consultant who advised on the Fawley, Alcan and Scow agreements, preached his sermon on 'half-time Britain on half-pay' consistently, convincingly and to some effect. Economists had long studied the international comparative measures of productivity in despair.

Agreements sought to reduce levels of manning in two main ways. Firstly, by reducing the number of production workers or operators manning different parts of the plant. Secondly, by abolishing such traditional institutions as mates for fitters, or maintenance workers. Each of these two types of reduction required greater flexibility.

(c) *Flexibility and Reducing Restrictive Practices.* One of the chief requirements for reducing hours of working and levels of manning was greater flexibility in all sections of the workforce. As far as production workers or process operators were concerned this meant learning about and being able to operate a wider range of the process rather than just a small specific section of the process. It also meant that operatives would be able to do simple maintenance tasks, 'use tools' instead of, for instance, waiting for a skilled craftsman to undo a nut. Flexibility for craftsmen meant some inter-craft flexibility: i.e. members of one craft carrying out the more straightforward tasks that were formerly restricted to another craft. In some cases this produced very dramatic changes in which, for instance, a job that required six men is now being carried out by one. On the other hand, this tends to be the area in which slowest progress is made.[9]

These then were the three main prongs of the early drive for productivity agreements: the reduction or eradication of overtime, a reduction in levels of manning, greater flexibility between operators and craftsmen and among craftsmen. In addition to these three main general goals some agreements also sought to make more specific changes, particularly to their organizations; to simplify and rationalize complex systems of payment and grading, and in general to bring sense, order and control to the organization and remuneration of the workforce.

In exchange for agreeing to these changes employees were given increased earnings, shorter hours and improved conditions of employment, including longer holidays, sickness pay, more secure tenure and longer periods of notice. In some cases this was specifically designed to eliminate the traditional distinctions and barriers between staff and works employees.

These early agreements were all made in capital intensive continuous process industries. This has led to the suggestion that productivity bargaining is most appropriate[10] or even only appropriate to this type of industry and technology at a particular point in time,[11] for two reasons. Firstly, it is capital intensive. Labour costs represents a low proportion of total costs but the proportion that, in the short term, is the most accessible to cost reduction by local management, because they are a high proportion of the costs that can be influenced without further massive new capital investment. Secondly, it is suggested that apart from the level of capital intensity, the form of the basic process and technology, and the type of workforce organization and system of payment that it requires or permits, make it particularly or uniquely appropriate to one type of productivity bargaining. For instance, production work in the process industry is like few other kinds of work, certainly at manual worker levels. It involves monitoring the

---

[9] Allan Flanders, *op. cit.* (1964).

[10] See British Rail's comments in Research paper No. 4 (*op. cit.*, 1967).

[11] A. B. Cherns, 'The Donovan Report and Associated Research Papers', *Occupational Psychology*, Vol. 42, No. 4, Oct. 1968.

production process and making such adjustments as are required to keep the process on specification, or to readjust it to meet new specifications. This involves long periods when the process is running normally, when nothing needs to be done. And yet there is always the possibility of a crisis that might mean untold danger, damage, loss and cost. In this situation it is very difficult to establish the 'right' level of manning as between the number required during normal operation and those required to deal with crises. Moreover, the contribution of the individual worker to the total volume of production is impossible to determine and is certainly unrelated to his 'effort' in any physical meaning of the word; indeed, his effort may well be inversely related to production where production is highest when he is doing least, during normal operations, and lowest when he is doing most, during crises, shut-downs or start-ups. Thus the measurement of work and the determination of appropriate levels of manning are very difficult, and any individual payment by results system impossible. It is not surprising if levels of manning and over-time become out of hand in these circumstances when the appropriate levels are so difficult to determine in absolute terms. Moreover, the size of the work force is small and its organization simple, compared to, say, a large engineering works. Despite the fact that there may be large numbers of craft unions, there are basically a group of production and process workers who monitor and adjust the process, and a group of maintenance workers or craftsmen who service, maintain and repair the plant. Once attention and application are given to the organization of the workforce, inherited and evolved from the requirements of very different types of technology, then ways in which it could be reorganized to reduce the time spent on jobs, and levels of manning are readily apparent.

It is presumably for these reasons it has been suggested that productivity bargaining was appropriate only to the oil, chemical, electricity generating and similar industries in the circumstances in which they found themselves by the end of the 1950s. Presumably again, the implication is that all they needed to do was to 'buy themselves out of trouble' with one big package productivity deal and then they could forget about productivity bargaining. We now know that these arguments, or at least the conclusions drawn from them, are not valid. It may be that the distinctive features of capital intensive, continuous-process based industry help to explain why the present trend towards productivity bargaining started there. It may also be true that these distinctive features of process technology have a critical impact on the form, content and consequences of the bargaining and the bargaining process and on its impact upon workers' jobs, job satisfaction and inter-group and inter-personal relationships. One of the most important areas of growth in industrial sociology during the past fifteen years has been an increasing awareness of the importance of technology and its impact on, and implications for, all aspects of an organization's structure and operations: on management structure and organization, on work group structure and character, on patterns of supervision, on workers' involvement and alienation, and on disputes, grievance-bargaining and industrial relations. If technology is so important in all these aspects of organization, then it will clearly be important in terms of the form and impact of productivity bargaining.

But as far as the concept of productivity bargaining is concerned we now know that it has a far more general relevance. Successful productivity agreements have been negotiated in labour intensive, service industries like British Rail and the GPO. Indeed, productivity bargains have been made across the full range of industries and technologies and have included white-collar workers as well as skilled, semi-skilled and unskilled blue-collar workers.[12] Organizations that pioneered the major productivity package deals have engaged in 'second generation' agreements because of the demands of technological innovation, because they subsequently perceived the opportunity for further advances in the use of manpower, or because they had consciously designed the original agreement to pave the way for a second one.

[12] See B. Towers and T. G. Whittingham, *The New Bargainers: A Symposium on productivity bargaining*. Department of Adult Education, Nottingham University, 1970, p. 33, for an account of the proportion of agreements concluded in each type of industry.

Beyond the Effort Bargain

If the immediate aim of an agreement is to restrain or reduce labour costs, thereby increasing labour productivity, the obvious and simple measure of their success is whether they fulfil these ends. A striking feature of the picture of the early agreements presented in the research paper for the Donovan Commission is the absence of such simple measures. It is beyond the scope of this study to explore the more specifically economic consequences. It must suffice to quote the conclusion of the NBPI review that three-quarters of the agreements studied have resulted in a reduction in costs per unit of output, reductions ranging from 7 to 15 per cent.

But alongside these less direct costs, the agreement will also have indirect effects; on the attitude and expertise of managers, or the attitudes and job satisfactions of operators, on the jobs of shop stewards and on the institutions and climate of industrial relations. As these features are critical to the health, growth and effectiveness of any enterprise, it can be argued that the effects that the process of productivity bargaining has on them can be as important, if not more important than any short-term productivity increase intrinsic to the actual bargain. If it significantly enhances the expertise and effectiveness of managers at all levels; if it improves the quality of industrial relations and makes the practice and institution of industrial relations more appropriate to circumstances and needs; and if it restructures the jobs of workers in ways that increase their involvement and satisfactions in their jobs, then it will have produced benefits of such value that they would warrant a short-term loss on the agreement itself, a loss that would be regarded as a valuable and important investment. If, on the other hand, the process of bargaining and the implementation of the agreement causes significant and permanent damage to these aspects of an organization, no short-term saving will compensate for this. For instance, there is little doubt that in some cases 'piece-work' or 'payment by results' schemes have increased productivity in the short term only at the expense of long-term costs, because in focusing on the wage-effort bargain, many motivational and organizational factors were neglected. It could be that productivity bargains, which are similar in that they link 'work' to 'wages', even though through a different mechanism, could suffer from similar long-term costs. This remains to be seen. But early writers on productivity bargaining have generally argued that it has a positive rather than a negative impact on the less directly economic areas.

Management and Supervisory Attitudes

Barbara Shenfield reports[13] that in the cases she studied, top management considered that the benefits in management education which resulted from the negotiations were so substantial and widespread that these alone would have justified the entire exercise. It is claimed that the negotiation and implementation focuses management's attention on the use of manpower and human resources, induces cost consciousness by providing new indices of performance and by introducing new methods of measuring work, productivity and performance. It recognizes and emphasizes managerial responsibility for industrial relations and brings a far wider range of managers into the process.[14]

On the other hand, such negotiations raise considerable problems for supervisors. Shenfield found that supervisors were the most dissatisfied group in her case-study. Essentially they felt that they had been treated inequitably. Workers had been given massive pay rises because, as supervisors saw it, they had been inefficient, unco-operative and lazy. Supervisors who had always given the company complete loyalty, unquestioning co-operation, and unrestrained effort had gained nothing out of it. Moreover, while their differentials had been whittled away, and their loyalty gone unrecognized and unrewarded, the problems and responsibilities in their jobs had increased. Flanders came to similar conclusions in his Fawley study.[15] He observes that although top management could be seen to be fully committed to the changes this was less true of middle managers and supervisors. In particular, replies to a questionnaire completed after the agreement was operating, showed

---

[13] Barbara Shenfield, *The Responsibilities of Company Boards* (provisional title), forthcoming, 1971.
[14] See also NBPI Report No. 36, *op. cit.* (1967).
[15] Allan Flanders, *op. cit.* (1964).

that nearly as many supervisors thought that the old organization had been better than the new, as took the alternative view. This was despite the fact that they themselves had benefited substantially from the agreement.

This is exactly what we would predict if supervisors and managers adhere to what Fox[16] calls a 'unitary' or teamwork concept of the industrial enterprise as being a team in which everybody should work together for the common good. Productivity bargaining recognizes that there are conflicts of interest in an industrial enterprise, particularly in terms of the supply and remuneration of labour, and that the only way of resolving this conflict is by negotiation. For the manager characterized by the teamwork concept, however, this is anathema. Employees *should* give full co-operation and effort. Inefficiency and restrictive practices are disloyal and wrong. For management then to go on and increase wages in return for changing work practices is to reward wrong-doing. If this concept is widespread among supervisors and managers then one would expect widespread lack of enthusiasm for productivity bargaining among them.

And according to Len Neal[17] this is exactly what happens. 'Anybody about to consider productivity bargaining ought to realize and keep on remembering that the opposition to productivity bargaining will probably come more from management than the trade unions . . . there is a too familiar misconception that everything would be all right if we would only change TU attitudes and the attitudes of manual workers. It is much more . . . a matter of changing management attitudes.' He concludes from this that a massive programme of management education and re-education, about the effective use of manpower, about human behaviour and motivation in industry and about techniques of work measurement is necessary *before* productivity bargaining can be successful and effective. This stands in marked contrast to the general argument on the management education benefits of productivity deals which sometimes gives the impression that management

---

[16] The Donovan Report, Research paper No. 3, Alan Fox, *Industrial Sociology and Industrial Relations*.

[17] D. C. Alexander (ed.), *A Productivity Bargaining Symposium;* Engineering Employees Federation Research Series (1969).

education is an automatic pay-off rather than an essential pre-requisite.

Industrial Relations and Worker Involvement

It has also been claimed that productivity bargaining has beneficial effects on the climate and institutions of industrial relations and on the attitudes and involvement of workers. It recognizes that major industrial relations decisions are taken at plant level, and strengthens and enhances the quality of industrial relations by increasing the frequency and range of plant consultation. Moreover, workers and work-groups are much more directly involved in decisions, thus strengthening industrial democracy. Furthermore, such changes normally mean that workers are given an opportunity to exercise abilities more fully, which in turn contributes to an increase in job satisfaction. Finally, it highlights deficiencies in trade-union organization and expertise, and encourages them to repair deficiencies in staff and supporting services.[18]

But the rationale behind productivity bargaining rests on a number of more fundamental propositions about industrial relations. Firstly, there is the now very familiar and widely accepted proposition that became enshrined in the Donovan Commission. 'Britain has two systems of industrial relations. The one is the formal system embodied in the official institutions. The other is the informal system created by the actual behaviour of trade unions and employers' associations, of managers, shop stewards, and workers.'

Local productivity bargaining at plant level is one form of what the commission saw as an answer to the damaging gap between the formal and informal systems. The informal system was out of control; out of management control and out of the control of workers' formal representatives. Custom and practice developed by default. Restrictive uses of labour, institution-alized overtime and phoney 'incentive' schemes, for instance, flourished in a situation where there was no formal machinery for controlling them. The solution that it offered was to recognize and formalize the informal system and to accept and encourage

---

[18] See NBPI Report No. 36, Allan Flanders, *op. cit.*, and B. Towers and T. G. Whittingham, *op. cit.*

the growth of formal collective bargaining at local levels covering a wider range of issues within formal written agreements that had hitherto been covered in national agreements—replacing fragmentary bargaining by comprehensive plant or company agreements.

The productivity bargain, extending negotiation to cover methods of working as well as rates of pay, is a conscious example of just this type of local plant bargaining This is directly in line with Flanders's argument that it is only at plant levels that the detailed analysis and specification of change in methods of working can be carried out. Moreover, he would argue that it is only at plant level that the detailed and extended negotiation, consultation, explanation, communication with and persuasion of union officers, shop stewards and work groups is possible.[19]

Conflict or Co-operation

The second major proposition that underlies the concept of productivity bargaining is that there is an inherent conflict of interests in industrial enterprises between management and employees. It is management who settle the terms and conditions of employment in concerns on behalf of capital. The third proposition, that follows from this, is that the *only* way to bring about reform and changes such as are sought through productivity agreements, and which will disturb balanced interests, is by engaging in collective bargaining to maintain or restore an acceptable balance of interests.[20]

This more extreme view may be, and has been, challenged. Other methods of tackling under-employment and increasing productivity have been tried, with some success. These include not only modifications to the wage-effort bargain in terms of 'payment by results' schemes, but also changes in the context and content of people's jobs divorced from the wage-work bargain (job-enlargement and job-enrichment); and human relations programmes involving changes in the styles and patterns of supervision and management. The main critics of the 'human relations' approach have argued partly on empirical grounds that such strategies are perceived as manipulative and

[19] Allan Flanders, *op. cit.*   [20] *Ibid.*, and Alan Fox, *op. cit.*

are ineffective,[21] and partly on moral grounds. Flanders, by inference, strongly condemns such approaches as 'treating the workers . . . as objects, to be cajoled where they cannot be coerced, and has not even the merit of honesty'.[22] Productivity bargaining, then, is seen as an expression of industrial democracy, and as both the only effective and the only moral way to reconcile the basic conflict between the two sides in industry.

Crucial to this aspect of the debate then is the empirical question as to what extent the 'conflict' model is actually held by workers. When workers are confronted with the teamwork versus pluralism (conflict) view, surprisingly they frequently accept the teamwork model. Thus, when Goldthorpe presented his car workers with the alternative, 77 per cent said 'basically on the same side'. This was in an industry currently racked by strikes. Moreover, the source of the common interest they identified was largely economic. They argued that the security and growth of their earnings was dependent on the visibility and growth of the enterprise. This did not mean that they were not conscious of any conflict of interest. The large majority thought their employer could pay them more and that their rate fixing was inequitable.

Similar findings resulted from a similar question to operatives in a petro-chemical plant.[23] What was striking here was that, although the objective sources and the overt symptoms of conflict are much less than in the motor-car industry, there was a more marked awareness of basic conflict. Fifty-eight per cent said that management and workers were basically on the same side compared to the 77 per cent in the Luton study. Nevertheless, over half still accepted the teamwork concept. But what was interesting was that 23 per cent did not accept the assumptions of the question and argued that in some circumstances they were on opposite sides, while in others they worked as a team. In particular they differentiate between the work situation and remuneration: 'on the job we work as a team, when it comes to money we're on different sides'. This distinction was emphasized by the way men without exception said that they thought the firm could pay

[21] For a discussion of this view, see C. Argyris, *Integrating the Individual and the Organization.*

[22] Allan Flanders, *op. cit.*, p. 200.   [23] Work in progress at Bath University.

them more, but at the same time agreed that they were under no pressure from management in their work.

Such evidence suggests that the approach to industrial relations in general and productivity bargaining in particular, needs to be more complex than either the conflict view or the human relations approach would indicate. Little progress can be made until the wage-work bargain is right. But little can be achieved by trying to regulate conduct wholly by rules, however arrived at. All that the formal agreement can do is to provide a framework within which attitudes and practices can be changed. The motivation for the change in attitudes and the use of discretion which are necessary to make the agreement work as intended must come from elsewhere. Moreover, there is an ample literature on the ingenuity which is exercised to assert the autonomy of the individual against the organization.[24] What is being increasingly realized is not that some measure of industrial democracy is a moral ideal, but that it is a fact, in the sense that workers inevitably have a say in what they do. The issue is simply the form which participation can most effectively take.[25] If, then, we recognize the limits of formal control, the motivations of the individual take on an increased significance.

Motivation and Productivity

We come then to what is, in a sense, the crucial question. What motivates men not simply to go to work, but more importantly, to work to the best of their ability—to exercise skill, responsibility and effort? One major influence behind the agreement which is the main subject of this study was the work of a number of behavioural and social scientists which has a direct bearing on this question. In recent years, the work of both psychologists and sociologists has converged to focus on the meaning, rewards, and deprivations of work in industrial society. To understand fully the implications of the current study, we must look first at the work of the social and behavioural scientists which had such an important bearing on the productivity agreement which we here analyse.

[24] F. E. Katz, *Autonomy and Organization: the Limits of Social Control* (1968).
[25] See Kenneth Walker, *Industrial Democracy, Fantasy, Fiction or Fact?* (Times Management Lecture, 1970).

Chapter 2

MEN AND MACHINES

Work and Human Nature

A basic problem for the management of any human enterprise is a correct diagnosis of what leads individuals to behave the way they do. Committal to prison for theft, fines and disqualifications for drinking and driving, liberal or tough divorce laws—all assume that human behaviour may be modified by what can be broadly categorized as incentives or disincentives.

The regulation and organization of behaviour in the industrial work-place is no exception. Indeed, it is here that there is at least as much systematic and conscious effort as in most other areas of human activity. And it is here that deficiencies in our understanding are often so painfully obvious. Beginning with the early investigations into industrial fatigue, through the era of scientific management and human relations, to the more recent notions of job enlargement and job enrichment, we have not only a wide variety of theories about the optimum method of organizing work, but also a changing set of assumptions and hunches about the motivation to work,[1] and indeed, about human nature itself.

To take but one example, the scientific management school associated with the work of Frederick Taylor assumed the primacy of economic motives—that men would seek to maximize their incomes with minimum physical effort. The monuments to Taylorism are piece-work and time-and-motion study. By these devices, quanta of effort were closely related to discrete increments in pay, and patterns of movements were studied to eliminate wasted effort. But men are more complex than this. And piece-work and motion study have been

---

[1] For a more detailed guide to the literature, see G. Hutton, *Thinking About Organization* (1969).

dethroned from the once eminent place they held in the management repertoire.[2]

The important point which we wish to make here is that all human interactions are based on assumptions and expectations about the responses of others. In most situations, we get by. Long familiarity with wives and husbands, friends and colleagues equips us with rule of thumb guide-lines. But the history of industrial management is the story of constantly changing theories and assumptions. And the study which we are about to report is no exception. From its inception, this was conceived as more than a straight effort bargain, in which money would be bargained for output. As in large sections of British industry today, management was aware of the recent work of social and behavioural scientists, about the motivation to work, the meaning of work and its satisfactions and dissatisfactions. The work of Likert, McGregor, and especially Herzberg,[3] had profoundly influenced their thinking and permeated the whole approach to the productivity bargain. Above all, they had been impressed by the arguments of Frederick Herzberg that money is seldom a source of positive satisfaction, that what motivates achievement is the chance to realize some aspect of the self, some skill or capacity.

Now, as we have seen, some of the strategies adopted by management have been found to rest on faulty or inadequate assumptions. Not only may the cost to industry be high, but the social cost to society through human dissatisfaction and impaired mental health may be greater than is often realized.[4] Work on the assembly line is among the most hated of all forms of work.[5] Yet it was introduced on the basis of what were seen as common-sense assumptions about breaking work down into simple components so that it can be easily learned, and be performed by those with little skill or training. But the assembly-line syndrome of boredom, and the subordination of man to

[2] See, for example, W. Brown, *Piecework Abandoned* (1962).

[3] R. Likert, *New Patterns of Management* (1961). D. McGregor, *The Human Side of Enterprise* (1960). F. Herzberg, *Work and the Nature of Man* (1969). For a particularly useful discussion of the literature on the organization of individuals, see C. Argyris, *Integrating the individual and the organization* (1964).

[4] A. Kornhauser, *Mental Health of Industrial Workers* (1965).

[5] See, for example, C. R. Walker and R. H. Guest, *The Man on the Assembly-line* (1952). R. Blauner, *Alienation and Freedom: The Factory Worker and His Industry* (1964).

the machine is the unintended consequence bequeathed by an era whose knowledge of human behaviour was much more limited and whose confidence in their understanding of it so much the more certain.

What distinguishes the exercise reported here is not simply the influence of the more recent theories from the social and behavioural sciences. Management were also anxious to check their assumptions and predictions. It was for this reason that the University was approached to provide a detached and objective monitoring of the exercise. Such a check is of interest not only to management, but also to the behavioural scientist. And since theories of motivation are so central to this inquiry, we begin by a detailed examination of the more recent work in this field, which provided the background to the agreement.

Motivation and Needs

One of the greatest difficulties in any attempt to come to grips with the complexity of human motivation is the great diversity of opinions which exist. Consequently, various theories aiming at some kind of synthesis have emerged. Coleman,[6] for example, has argued that all of man's motives can be viewed as serving one or both of two basic purposes: self-maintenance, and growth towards the actualization of his potentialities. Maintenance directed behaviour attempts to satisfy both biological and psychological needs. Coleman includes in his list of biological or body needs four different groups; visceral (food, water, oxygen, sleep); safety; sex; sensory and motor. In the last group he includes a need for sensory stimulation and he reports (1960, p. 118):

'If incoming stimulation is greatly reduced for a period of several hours, an individual's thought processes become disoriented and he begins to have hallucinations. After a prolonged period without sensory stimulation, performance on intelligence and other psychological tests is temporarily lowered and time is necessary to restore normal mental functioning.'[7]

[6] J. C. Coleman, *Personality Dynamics and Effective Behaviour* (1960).
[7] See also R. Cooper, 'Alienation from Work', *New Society*, January 30, 1969, pp. 161–3, and W. Heron, 'The pathology of boredom', *Scientific American*, 1957, 196 (1), pp. 52–6.

Coleman believes that 'striving towards maintenance' include not only bodily processes but also psychological. There are five of these: 'a meaningful picture of our world and our place in it', security, feelings of belonging and approval, a sense of personal worth and warm, accepting interpersonal relationships. Maintenance motivation is also described as deficiency motivation by Coleman.

Managers who accept this tension reduction model of employee behaviour are apparently making a number of assumptions about human motivations.[8] They seem to believe that workers can only be motivated by economic incentives; that they are passive agents to be manipulated, motivated and controlled by the manager; that they are inherently lazy and only activated by external incentives, i.e. money, and even then only when they need it to buy goods or to pay the rent. According to this management view, workers come to work 'for what they can get out of it', or 'just for the money'. These assumptions have been sharply criticized by some social scientists and more recently by managers themselves. White puts it neatly: 'Even when its primary needs are satisfied and its homeostatic chores are done, an organism is alive, active and up to something'.[9] Cofer and Appley[10] present a 'need reduction' or 'equilibration' model, represented thus: deprivation (tension increase)—action—satisfaction (tension decrease).

But maintenance or deficiency motivation cannot explain the behaviour of the man 'who throws himself into his work with zest and enthusiasm'. Coleman regards these actions as expressions of 'actualization strivings'. For him, the essence of actualization is growth—physical, intellectual, emotional and spiritual. These strivings take five forms: increased satisfaction in one's experience, self-enhancement, the development of one's capacities, becoming a 'real' person, 'creating new linkages with one's world'. This last one is 'not the deficiency motivated love of the affection-starved child which is possessive, jealous and insatiable, but an outgoing love, accepting of others as they are and concerned with their needs'. Coleman believes

[8] E. H. Schein, *Organisational Psychology* (1966).
[9] R. W. White, 'Motivation Reconsidered: The Concept of Competence', *Psychological Review*, 1959, 66, 297–333.
[10] C. N. Cofer and M. H. Appley, *Motivation Theory and Research* (1964).

that actualization strivings, like maintenance directed behaviour, form a regular pattern: arousal—energy mobilization—goal directed behaviour—feelings of satisfaction. But satisfaction comes through increased effort, activity and stimulation rather than the removal of tension or the reduction of needs. He holds that there is an interaction between self-maintenance and self-actualization strivings in that the latter may not appear if the former remain unsatisfied, but also that actualization may take precedence over the supposedly more basic maintenance requirements. This is the explanation of the behaviour of 'the scientist who may go without food and sleep, in the excitement of a crucial experiment'.

The Hierarchy of Needs

This view of human motivation, that there are biological maintenance needs, psychological maintenance needs and actualization needs, is essentially that of A. H. Maslow.[11] He assumes a hierarchy of basic needs with self-actualization at the top, and holds that for the higher needs to function there must have been a prior satisfaction of the lower needs. At the base of the hierarchy are the physiological needs like hunger and thirst.

> 'For the man who is extremely and dangerously hungry no other interests exist but food. He dreams food, he remembers food, he thinks about food, he emotes about food, he perceives only food and he wants only food.'[12]

The non-satisfaction of other physiological needs has been investigated experimentally more recently than food deprivation. Recently there have been a number of experiments on sleep deprivation in which individual subjects have remained awake for two hundred hours or more. Almost invariably it has been found that after some one hundred hours without sleep there ensues a progressive disintegration of personality and rational behaviour. Paranoid symptoms emerge in which

[11] A. H. Maslow, *The Psychological Review*, 1943, 50, 370–96.
[12] 'One developed a compulsion to steal pots and pans; others collected menus; pin-ups of food replaced the other variety; and a few subjects decided to become chefs or farmers.'—Franklin, *et. al.*, 'Observations on human behaviour in experimental semi-starvation and rehabilitation', *J. Clin. Psychol.*, 1948, 4, 28–45.

the subject may, for example, accuse the experimenters of trying to ruin his attempt to remain awake for the prescribed period.[13]

Next in Maslow's hierarchy are the safety needs which, if unsatisfied, may also dominate behaviour. According to this view, workers preoccupied with job security because of, for example, redundancy fears, will be unable or unwilling to concern themselves with any other aspect of the work situation and indeed, at home, may appear to be unable to cope with family demands.

If both the physiological and the safety needs are fairly well gratified, Maslow argues, it becomes possible for the next need stage to be reached. Now the individual is aware of, and can pay attention to, his needs for love and affection and belongingness:

> 'Now the person will feel keenly as never before, the absence of friends, or a sweetheart or a wife or children. He will hunger for affectionate relations with people in general, namely for a place in his group, and he will strive with great intensity to achieve this goal. He will want to attain such a place more than anything else in the world and may even forget that once, when he was hungry, he sneered at love as unreal or unnecessary or unimportant.'[14]

The esteem needs are the next to appear in the hierarchy. These include self-respect and the respect of others. The satisfactions of these lead to feelings of self-confidence and personal worth. These needs are the last of the deficiency needs in Maslow's hierarchy. Before self-actualization needs can occur the physiological, safety, love and esteem needs must have been 'largely gratified'. These 'basically satisfied people' are now ready to become 'self-actualizers'.

Self-actualization

Though in Maslow's view 'basically satisfied people are the exception, we do not know much about self-actualization,

[13] R. Wilkinson, 'Sleep and Dreams', in B. M. Foss, *New Horizons in Psychology* (Penguin Books, 1966).
[14] A. H. Maslow, *Motivation and Personality* (1954).

either experimentally or clinically', he has, in fact, made many contributions to the controversy which this concept has aroused. He has, for example, argued the case for distinguishing between behaviour motivated by deficiency needs and that motivated by growth needs (self-actualization).[15] In the growth-directed self-actualizing worker, gratification increases rather than decreases motivation; i.e. self-actualization is itself rewarding. The satisfaction of growth motivation leads to health whereas the satisfaction of deficiency needs only prevents illness. The kinds of behaviour to be expected when a worker is motivated by growth needs are very different from those that are shown by workers motivated by attempts to satisfy deficiency needs:

'When we examine people who are predominantly growth-motivated, the coming-to-rest conceptions of motivation becomes completely useless. In such people, gratification breeds increased rather than decreased motivation, heightened rather than lessened excitement. The appetites become intensified and heightened. They grow upon themselves and instead of wanting less and less such a person wants more and more, for instance, education. The person rather than coming to rest, becomes more active.'

Another difference between the two types of people is in their dependence on or independence of their environment. Maslow argues that 'the deficiency-motivated man must be more afraid of his environment since there is always the possibility that it may fail or disappoint him. In contrast, the self-actualizing individual by definition, gratified in his basic needs, is far less dependent, far less beholden, far more autonomous and self-directed'.

These views have markedly influenced other social scientists such as Herzberg. But they have not been without their critics. Cofer and Appley[16] accept that there is some evidence that intense physiological and safety needs can dominate behaviour but,

[15] A. H. Maslow, 'Deficiency Motivation and Growth Motivation' in Jones (ed.), *Nebraska Symposium on Motivation* (1955).
[16] C. N. Cofer and M. H. Appley, *op. cit.* (1964).

C

'the emphasis on self-actualization suffers in our opinion from the vagueness of its concepts, the looseness of its language and the inadequacy of the evidence related to its major contentions. It is difficult to see how it can foster meaningful investigations in view of its vague language. The first prerequisite for further development and evaluation of this viewpoint, it seems to us, is the formulation of the important ideas in language that is relatively precise. It may then be possible to carry out investigations related to these basic premises.'

Motivators and Satisfiers

Herzberg would claim that he has now made it possible to do this.[17] His motivation-hygiene theory states that there is one set of factors which leads to positive job satisfaction and another set which, while not involved in positive satisfaction, is sufficient to arouse job dissatisfaction. Both set of factors meet the needs of employees but it is primarily the former (i.e. the motivators) which bring about the kind of job satisfaction and the kind of improvement in the performance of work skills which managers ask of their employees. These are the equivalent of Maslow's self-actualization factors, while those that prevent or end job dissatisfaction are equivalent to Maslow's four lower-order need system. In Herzberg's theory these are the hygiene factors. In short, he argues that every human being has two categories of needs: avoidance of deprivation and achievement of potentiality. The first category which represents the 'Adam view of man' includes the 'avoidance of loss of life, hunger, pain and sexual deprivation' and the learned fears that become attached to these primary needs. The second category, which represents the 'Abraham concept of the human being, is man's compelling urge to realize his own potentiality by continuous psychical growth'.

What happens if these needs are met at work? If they are in the first category the result will be the avoidance of job dissatisfaction and if they are in the second category the result will be positive job satisfaction. The factors which prevent or end job dissatisfaction are the major environmental aspects of work (i.e. the 'job context' factors). Those factors which

[17] F. Herzberg, *Work and the Nature of Man* (1968).

produce positive attitudes to work and 'motivate the individual to superior performance and effort', are, Herzberg claims, achievement, recognition, work itself, responsibility and advancement. They are 'job content' factors and they provide opportunities for self-actualizing growth. So work and working conditions can satisfy the 'hygiene' needs without satisfying the 'growth' needs. Only if these latter find opportunities for expression at work will a high level of motivation result. It is possible that the theory allows for workers to be non-dissatisfied and non-motivated. It is also possible apparently for workers to be dissatisfied but motivated since in one study reported by Herzberg half of a group of workers with 'poor hygiene morale' received an increase in 'motivators' and half (the controls) did not. After six months there were improvements in morale scores and in work performance. Herzberg also argues that it is possible for workers not to have any 'growth' needs or at least not active ones. These 'hygiene-seekers' show little interest in the kind and quality of the work they do. They are basically avoidance-oriented workers only affected by the job-context variables of supervisor-employee interaction, company policy and administration, working conditions, inter-personal relationships with peers, wages, job security and status. Even when all these are favourable and dissatisfaction is minimal for the time being, there is no guarantee that these workers are ready for the 'motivators' or that they will not be complaining about the dissatisfiers in six months' time. Therefore if a motivator, such as the chance to control their own work were introduced, 'some workers would markedly improve their work performance whilst some would deteriorate to a certain extent as they failed for reasons of personal adjustment or of skill to meet the challenge of freedom'.

Managers have a responsibility, according to Herzberg's view of their role, not only to arrange for the effective use of hygiene factors, as this remains necessary, but at the same time to develop their employees so that they can achieve psychological growth, become self-actualizers and responsive to the 'motivators'. In addition they have the vital task of recognizing the motivator-oriented workers so that they are not managed as if they were 'hygiene-seekers'. Job enlargement would be one important change, if it provided for psychological growth, which for Herzberg means 'the opportunities to increase knowledge, understanding, creativity, to experience ambiguity in decision making and finally to individuate and seek real growth'.[18]

The Theories Tested

These propositions have been tested empirically by Herzberg himself in an investigation involving two hundred engineers and accountants in Pittsburgh,[19] in another study using 'lower-level supervisors representing a wide range of industries in Finland' and by other investigators in the United States, Hungary and Russia. In these replications the 'basic motivation-hygiene interview' was used or one with only minor modifications; for instance, in one study (Herzberg, 1968, p. 132).

'a total of three hundred and seventy-three third-level supervisors completed a lengthy questionnaire, part of which required them to report two incidents in response to each of the following questions: (1) "Occasionally something happens to the (title of job) that makes him feel particularly well satisfied with his job, and that stimulates him to contribute even more. Think of the most recent time something like this has happened to you." (2) "Occasionally something interferes with the (title of job) efforts to carry out his job effectively. Think of the most recent time you experienced this kind of frustration." '

Herzberg's method for analysing and coding the interviews was used in these replications. In each of them the job factors predicted by the theory to cause dissatisfaction were generally speaking in the hygiene factors list or similar to Herzberg's items. In the study reported above, for example:

'The major factors that led to negative job feelings were ill-advised management decisions, ham-stringing procedures or red-tape, union activities, poor co-operation from independent groups, management apathy towards problems or needs, delay or incomplete instructions and information,

[18] F. Herzberg, *Work and the Nature of Man* (1969).
[19] F. Herzberg, *et. al.*, *The Motivation to Work* (1959).

interference in management of one's own operations, being by-passed in decisions affecting the job and having requests or recommendations turned down.'

Similarly, job factors predicted by the theory to produce 'positively motivating events' were, generally speaking, in the motivators list or similar to them. In the same study '37% of the positive events were listed under the factor of competence'[20] which Herzberg argues is essentially similar to his motivators.[21] The second major factor determining positive job satisfaction was 'a category named recognition for accomplishment . . . which is clearly similar to the Herzberg factor of recognition for achievement'.

The Russian replication led the investigators to stress the importance for worker motivation of the job content rather than the job context factors:

'The basic factor which imparts the greatest influence on the attitude to work is the content and character of the work itself.'

After reviewing all of these replications Herzberg claimed,

'Few studies in industrial psychology have been replicated as often as the motivation-hygiene study and the evidence appears to be overwhelming that the nature of job attitudes is reflected by the theory first proposed in "The Motivation to Work".'

One study appears to be similar in several respects to the one reported here in *The Nylon Spinners* and is therefore of particular interest. It is important because it brought 'the implications of the theory into active management thinking and practice'. This was carried out at the Texas Instruments Company of Dallas 'as part of a new orientation to industrial relations'. This Company started to investigate the motivation of its employees in 1958. By the end of 1960 it had become

[20] F. Herzberg, *op. cit.* (1959).
[21] See also, R. W. White, 'Motivation Reconsidered: The Concept of Competence', *Psychological Review*, 1959, 66, 297–333.

sufficiently interested in Herzberg's research to want to test the validity of his conclusions at T.I. In 1961 the Company study was started. The sample consisted of 282 employees; 50 scientists, 55 engineers, 50 manufacturing supervisors, 73 male hourly-paid technicians and 52 female hourly assemblers. A company interviewer asked each one of these subjects: 'Think of a time when you felt exceptionally good or exceptionally bad about your job, either your present job or any other job you have had. This can be either the "long-range" or the "short-range" kind of situation as I have just described it. Tell me what happened.' 'Long-range' was defined as 'strong feelings lasting more than two months', and 'short-range' less than two months. Some favourable and unfavourable responses to these interview questions are quoted by Myers[22] for each of the five job categories, e.g.:

'About six months ago I was given an assignment to develop a new product. It meant more responsibility and an opportunity to learn new concepts. I had to study and learn. It was an entirely different job. I had been in basic research where it's difficult to see the end results. Now I'm working much harder because I'm more interested.'

When all these interviews were coded it was reported that, 'the factors in the work situation which motivate employees are different from the factors that dissatisfy employees'. It was also found that responses which could be identified within the category of 'achievement' made up 33 per cent of the total responses from all five job categories. These achievement-oriented responses were reported twice as many times in the favourable as in the unfavourable experiences of the workers, i.e. 'achievement' was a 'motivator' and not a hygiene factor. But 'achievement' did not apparently mean the same thing to these five groups of workers. For the scientists it was closely associated with their job performance, i.e. work itself. For the supervisors it meant 'a stepping stone to success', while it derives its primary importance for the females 'from the affirmation it wins from her supervisor'. The conclusions drawn

[22] M. S. Myers, 'Who Are Your Motivated Workers?', *Harvard Business Review* (January–February, 1964).

38

from the study were thought to validate Herzberg's research and the ten-year plan for personnel administration was restructured in 1963 to fit motivation-maintenance theory concepts. Functions performed by personnel were analysed in terms of their potential for serving motivation or maintenance needs. Next, both the theory and the research on which it was based were thoroughly explained to managers and supervisors at all levels through the medium of large group meetings, at which they were informed of the Company's plans to implement the theory and their co-operation was elicited.[23]

Validation studies have also been carried out in British companies, including ICI.[24] They were testing Herzberg's hypothesis made in 1968 that 'job enrichment improves both task efficiency and human satisfaction'.[25] The five studies reported by Paul *et al.* seem to be trying to answer three main questions:

1. 'Can similarly positive results be obtained elsewhere with other people doing different jobs?'

2. 'Are there not situations where the operational risk is so high that it would be foolhardy to attempt to pass responsibility and scope for achievement down the line?'

3. 'In view of so many possible difficulties in the way, are the gains to be expected from job enrichment significant or only marginal?'

These studies were conducted with laboratory technicians, sales representatives, design engineers and factory supervisors. At the end of the experimental period, which 'generally lasted a year and was never less than six months' in each study, the investigators had produced evidence which seemed to indicate the following answers to the three questions:

1. Yes. 2. No ('Problems there are, but we have not encountered one.') 3. 'We believe the gains are significant.'

But we cannot understand the problems of the relations between men and machines simply by looking at the human side—at the needs and aspirations which men bring to their work. We must take account, too, of the characteristics of the

[23] Myers, 'Who Are Your Motivated Workers?'

[24] J. W. Paul, *et. al.*, 'Job Enrichment Pays Off', *Harvard Business Review*, March–April, 1969.

[25] F. Herzberg, 'One More Time: How Do You Motivate Employees?', *Harvard Business Review*, January–February, 1968.

machines on which they work—that is, the technology of production. The tasks which men perform are to a considerable extent shaped and determined by the technology. There are obviously significant differences in the tasks performed by a craftsman, compared with those of the man on the assembly-line, in levels of skill, and in the length of the job cycle. The relations between men and machines then, may usefully be thought of as a socio-technical system. And the socio-technical system of a craft technology, an assembly-line technology, or a process technology, will clearly each differ in significant ways; ways which have important implications for the motivations and satisfactions of the men on the machines.

The Socio-Technical System and Motivation

We are here exploring a particular socio-technical system. The fact that the technology involves the extrusion of molten polymer through fine holes to produce thread largely determines the tasks which men do. One of the characteristics of much modern machine technology, is the way in which the production process is broken up into distinct elements, so that the worker performs only a narrow range of tasks on a small part of the total product. Consequently his daily work is largely meaningless; he is unable to see the contribution which his activity makes to the total product. Moreover, the pace of work, the methods to be used, and the organization of the plan of work, are all decisions taken out of his hands, mainly by those who have designed the machine. In short, the worker is virtually powerless to exercise any control over the tasks he performs. Under such conditions, work ceases to be a form of self-expression and becomes primarily instrumental—a means to other ends; the worker becomes a *thing*—an appendage to the machine—in short alienated.[26] One of the most potent indices of such estrangement from the self is a heightened awareness of time. There is no involvement in the present; only an anticipation of the end of work, of release from the monotony and boredom, the heat, the noise and fumes.

[26] Blauner identifies four dimensions of alienation; powerlessness, meaninglessness, isolation and self-estrangement. For a more detailed discussion, see *op. cit.* (1964), Chapters 2 and 8.

Such studies of the relation between technology and the meaning and satisfaction of work focus attention on the characteristics of the production process and their significance. And although the vocabularies used by psychologists and sociologists differ, there is a substantial convergence of ideas. Blauner talks of alienation; but he does so in a way which is almost indistinguishable from Herzberg. 'When work provides opportunities for control, creativity, and challenge—when, in a word, it is *self-expressive*[27] and enhances an individual's unique potentialities—then it contributes to the worker's sense of self-respect and dignity. . . .'

But the technology is not the only determinant of the tasks men perform and of the daily conduct of their working lives. The precise allocation of tasks and the mode of their performance has still to be determined. And this is the function of the organization of work. Indeed, a major preoccupation of the literature on the management of industrial organizations is concerned with devising the most effective means of organization. What is particularly interesting is the growing awareness in such literature that the needs of individuals must be taken into account. Previously, emphasis was on devising strategies for decision-making and co-ordination. The general outcome of such strategies was dependence and submissiveness which increased as one went down the chain of command. The result was not only the lack of opportunities for self-actualization, but the generation of a variety of *strategies of independence* as a protection against organizational demands.[28]

Side by side then with the increasing awareness of the importance of motivation there has been a growing literature emphasizing the need to increase involvement in the decision-making process at all levels, of which the most influential in industry has probably been R. Likert's *New Patterns in Management*. Participative group organization, to use Likert's term, 'tends to develop greater organizational flexibility, commitment, responsibility, effectiveness in problem solving . . .'.[29] In short, these are the organizational conditions necessary for

[27] Our italics. R. Blauner, *op. cit.* (1964), p. 37.
[28] For an account of the literature on goldbricking, rate, setting and the like, see C. Argyris, *op. cit.*, Chapter 4.
[29] *Ibid.*, p. 185.

'self-actualization'.[30] The technology leaves some room for manoeuvre. The way in which tasks are organized may be a key factor influencing the meaning and satisfaction of work.

What is particularly interesting about this experiment is the fact that the technology remained unchanged. The innovations were organizational ones. As we shall see later, such changes were of necessity limited, and could only take place within the parameters fixed by the production technology. Nevertheless this study will indicate the very considerable impact of such organizational changes, and can be interpreted as a challenge to any narrow view of technological determinism.

We need not spend long on describing the process itself, but a brief outline is necessary. The process starts from the charging floor where the polymer chips from which the yarn is made are loaded into hoppers. It is released from these to the unit floor where it is melted and whence it is pumped to the extrusion floor. Here it is extruded through dyes as molten filaments and air-cooled. On the spin-doff floor the yarn is wound on to cylinders. The process thus far described takes place mainly in the spinning section through which it passes in a continuous vertical stream. When it reaches the last floor it is doffed, or taken off the machine on cylinders. It is transported from here to the last major section, the drawtwist area, where it is wound on to bobbins. In the course of this operation it is stretched and twisted to make what is called true yarn. The auxiliary areas deal with inspection, low-grade yarn, residual yarn on cylinders, empty bobbins and cartons returned by customers, packing, warehousing, and so on.

For nearly all of the low-skilled operatives the work was characterized by a division of labour that allowed only for the repetitive performance of a limited set of standardized tasks. Moreover, particularly for spinning and drawtwist operatives, their work was organized for them to the extent of informing them on which machines to perform their tasks, the precise time to do this, and the time limits for carrying out the tasks. In the auxiliary areas operatives had to fulfil work quotas

[30] Such forms of organization are variously called 'Theory Y' (McGregor), 'organic' (Burns and Stalker), etc. They are characterized by the distribution of decision-making throughout the organization, an emphasis on co-operation, constant pressure to job enrichment and job enlargement, and decentralization of responsibility. See Argyris, *op. cit.* (1964), p. 185.

SPINNING

[To face page 42

'STRINGING UP' – DRAWTWIST AREA

either in teams or individually. Thus, virtually no scope was given for initiative or autonomy. The operatives were in a strait-jacket of standard practice and generally fairly tight supervision:

> 'It was all laid down as standard methods. You had a book more or less like a bible and it told you everything; how to fetch your steps, to position your steps, in order to change your cake' ('cake'—local term for Cylinder of yarn).

The Agreement

It is against this background that we must discuss the agreement which came into effect at the beginning of 1968. For the management at ICI, this was intended as more than a straight effort bargain. It was hoped that the changes in manning which were to be introduced would lead to job enlargement, and job enrichment and would thus result in more satisfying work, offering more scope for individual responsibility and initiative, and thus, for self-actualization.

It must be stressed that this is not an account of the actual process of bargaining. In this, it differs from the report of the Fawley agreements. We were called in to monitor the effect of the changes, mainly at shop floor level. And this is the primary emphasis of the report. Nevertheless, some account is necessary of the actual process of reaching the agreement, and of the changes which were introduced. It is to this that we turn in the next chapter.

Chapter 3

THE AGREEMENT

The actual process of bargaining took place at two main levels and in a series of stages. Firstly there were national discussions between the Company and the unions which resulted in an agreement to introduce trials of proposals for more effective manpower utilization in a number of plants together with changes in pay and conditions. At this level, discussions centred on the effort-bargain, in which increased flexibility between tradesmen and general workers would be exchanged for changes in pay and conditions. Secondly, there were the extensive discussions at plant level which aimed at achieving the maximum involvement by operatives in the changes.

The Company and the Unions

Discussions between the Company and the unions resulted in an agreement for trials in a number of sites. The sites chosen for the trials were designated centrally. The document to which Company and unions were signatories set out the aims of the exercise, including changes in manning aimed at greater flexibility and changes in employment conditions and salary structure.

The preamble stated that the common aim was to achieve and maintain the maximum efficiency in the Company's operations and that in pursuing this aim it is common ground:

'1. That an employee must be employed to the best of his ability for as much of his time as possible.

2. That an employee must be given the status and remuneration which will recognize the importance of his contribution to the Company and his acceptance of further responsibility.'

44

To achieve more effective use of manpower, it was agreed that operatives, with suitable training, could carry out less skilled craft tasks which formed only a subsidiary part of their work, and that tradesmen could do work of other trades which formed a subsidiary part of the main job of their own trade.

In exchange for these and other measures to increase flexibility, all employees covered by the agreement would be put on an annual salary paid weekly. There were to be eight salary levels, and each job would be assessed for salary level by three criteria; mental and personality requirements, physical requirements and acquired skills and knowledge. Rates of earnings for each grade were also fixed centrally. Local negotiations were restricted to agreeing job descriptions and to the grading of jobs. In addition, security of employment was to be improved by four weeks' notice of termination, and payment for sickness absence. Stability of salary was to be guaranteed under stated conditions. The agreement also included supplementary payments for shift and day rotas, overtime, and working conditions.

Plant Level Negotiations[1]

Thus far, it will be seen that the framework agreed between the company and the unions was strictly a wage-effort type agreement. Company policy, however, attached considerable importance to the implications of the work of behavioural and social scientists, particularly the work of Herzberg and Likert indicating the importance of motivation and participation. Only a small nucleus of senior management was entirely convinced, but all agreed that the ideas were worth a try, and that there was no point in being half-hearted if the application of such ideas were to have any chance of success.

A document prepared for the guidance of all personnel involved in the exercise began by stressing the need to create an atmosphere favourable to co-operation before negotiations could begin. In particular, talks should include discussions 'on motivation, presenting the theories of social scientists such as Herzberg and McGregor. . . . It is necessary for the ultimate success of the operation that, even at the opening stages, an

45

awareness of the concept that money is not the sole moti-vator must be present among the operatives.' Moreover, the ground was prepared by abolishing clocking-in and penalties for poor quality work some time before the agreement was introduced.

The actual process of negotiation involved setting up a number of working parties each concerned with one area of the plant. A typical working party would be chaired by the Assistant Works Manager and consisted of the Shift Manager, the Work Study Section Leader, Work Study Officer, Tech-nical Officer and Engineer. None would belong to the section whose work was being discussed, and none would be responsible for executive decisions in the section. In short, steps were taken to ensure that discussions would not be inhibited by talking to the 'boss'.

During the first phase, the task of the working parties was to collect information and establish the facts on costs, efficiency and work patterns. Areas for investigation were allocated to individuals or pairs who would then report back to formal meetings, pointing out flaws and deficiencies in current practice in order to stimulate discussion and encourage suggestions for change. In this way, the working parties were the main vehicle for detailed discussions with the shop floor, and acted as intermediaries with management in working out and imple-menting the details of the agreement.

The second phase began with the formation of shop-floor discussion groups, led by a foreman and consisting of a shop steward and two operatives, with two or more operatives who would attend one or more meetings only. It was emphasized that all men on the shop floor could have a say if they wished, either in person or through a representative. The final, and in some ways most important task of the discussion groups, was to write draft job descriptions. It was at these 'gel-sessions' that the future pattern of work was discussed, including proposals for transfer of jobs between craft and non-craft. At these sessions, a 'neutral' chairman was chosen, normally the Training Officer who had not previously been involved in negotiations. Management was not present. Job descriptions thus produced were finally negotiated with the company by a meeting of stewards.

46

Plant Democracy

It can be seen that the actual process of negotiations was itself part of a change in industrial relations. The emphasis throughout was on obtaining the full involvement of managers, supervisors and operatives at all levels. 'It may well be found that such a meeting (working party) is the first occasion on which interested parties have been brought together. . . .'

The emphasis too, was on real participation in the planning of change:

> 'Every effort must be made to resist the demand for a blue-print. At this stage, operatives are still suspicious of the motives behind the formation of the discussion groups and cannot readily accept that their views are being sought. They insist that "it has already been decided", so that their only function is the traditional one of criticising and searching for flaws. Or else, conditioned by suggestions schemes, they fear that their ideas are going to be wrested from them "for nothing". The importance of not presenting a blue-print is two-fold; firstly to gain acceptance of the idea that operatives should have a real chance of discussing their work amongst themselves and, by group discussion, proposing improvements; secondly, to provide an atmosphere free from the restricted horizon of a blue-print in which to develop alternatives superior to the working-party proposals. It must be clear at all times that the working-party proposals are open to modification: indeed it will probably be found that there are a number of respects in which the future pattern cannot emerge until operatives' views have been obtained.
>
> 'There must be feed-back of ideas from the discussion groups to the working party. These must be analysed for their merits, and bulletins issued to the discussion groups indicating points of agreements or difference, relative merits, and what action will be taken.'

It must be emphasized that this account of the actual process of the negotiations is 'second-hand', in the sense that we were not there to observe the events described. We began to observe the plant only a few months before the agreement

47

was implemented in January 1968. What is important is not what actually happened, but how events are *perceived* by those who were there. It is *their perceptions* of reality to which individuals respond. And on this we can say something, since it was precisely to monitor the process and find out what was actually happening, as distinct from what management hoped or expected would happen, that the University was approached. How the supervisors and the men on the shop floor actually *saw* the negotiations, and the meanings they attached to them, is described in Chapters 6 and 7.

What then, briefly, were the changes which resulted from the negotiations? The changes were of three main kinds: firstly, changes in the structure of industrial relations; secondly, organizational changes, or changes in the socio-technical system; and thirdly, changes in payment.

Structure of Industrial Relations

Before the agreement, there were two main structures channelling relations between management and men. On the one hand there was the Works Council, whose activities excluded anything relating to pay and conditions which were subject to union negotiation. Secondly, there were the unions and shop stewards. The main union is the T and G W whose branch secretary is a full-time employee responsible for all plant negotiations. Negotiations on behalf of craftsmen are conducted by the full-time district officer of the AEF, although he, in fact, was not much involved in the plant negotiations.

The new consultative machinery integrates the Works Council and the unions, and consists of selected members plus elected union representatives. There is a three-tier structure. At the basic grass-roots level are the foremen's discussion groups. Next there are the shift meetings, at which supervisors and shop stewards are present. The new Works Council is composed of twelve shop floor members plus eight from management. Any issue may be raised, but can be taken out and fed into the normal negotiating machinery if this is requested. One important spin-off from this integrated machinery is the very rapid communication which it makes possible right down to shop-floor level and without by-passing either unions or supervisors. Any important issue can be communicated to the shop floor within twenty-four hours via the shift meetings.

Organizational Changes

A major objective of the agreement was to achieve a re-organization of work so that the operative was subject to less detailed control by the rule book and by supervisors. Accordingly, supervision was reduced and much responsibility which was formerly borne by supervisors was transferred to operatives. The most important change here is that operatives now plan and organize their own work. For example, in the drawtwist area the system of working to a planned schedule has been replaced by a free-queuing system whereby operatives determine which machines to doff, string-up, or whatever the task may be. They also plan their own meal breaks and rest periods themselves. One result of this is an increasing independence of supervision so that, even though operatives generally consider that some foremen will be necessary in future in case of emergency and to give technical advice, they foresee drastic reductions.

In addition, there has been some job enlargement. Although proposals to add minor maintenance tasks to the operatives' jobs had not been agreed with the craft unions at the time of the inquiry most have since come into operation. The extent of these changes varies considerably from area to area, and it is evident on a broad view of the data that most change has occurred in the spinning area. Whereas formerly most operatives mainly worked in teams confined to either the extrusion or spin-doff floors, the teams are now organized vertically over three floors. Spinning operatives are now trained to work on any of these three levels with the object of creating greater flexibility of labour and consequently more efficient utilization of manpower. There is no job rotation scheme as such, but rather a movement of labour to where it is most needed, when it is needed. In fact, generally speaking, operatives still work mainly on one floor—on the tasks that they tend to be best at—switching from floor to floor or team to team if the necessity arises.

In the drawtwist area, operatives have been cross-trained to work on other drawtwist machines, although the differences

D

in technique are not great. They have taken over responsibility for machine scheduling previously determined by a computer. They also perform additional jobs such as packing bobbins directly into polythene bags (formerly done by auxiliary operatives). This involves inspecting the bobbin and taking complete responsibility for its condition when it reaches the customer. They now segregate cylinders according to the amount of residual yarn left on them preparatory to their being transported to auxiliary areas. In common with spinning operatives, they are now responsible for checking machinery—gears, draw ratios, etc.—but this is a relatively infrequent task for most workers.

In common with the above two areas, greater flexibility has been introduced into the auxiliary areas, resulting from the cross-training of operatives. Moreover, a good deal of rationalization has taken place making the co-ordination of work more efficient. Some jobs have been enlarged, combining hitherto separate tasks into one job.

Changes in Payment

One other major change introduced was more directly related to the role of direct monetary incentives. Before the agreement, an incentive scheme was in operation which functioned essentially in a negative way, in that a bonus was awarded and deductions made from it for mistakes leading to a lowering of the quality of the yarn. In order to enforce this scheme quality patrollers were employed to examine the work. For workers in the auxiliary area the system worked differently. Either in groups or individually, production quotas had to be met in order to earn the bonus. Production over this quota earned no extra bonus.

Under the new agreement this scheme was discarded in favour of a fixed annual salary paid weekly. This was done partly because it was assumed that since the worker's main concern was his weekly pick-up, and changing sections might mean losing money, there would be resistance to such changes. But more important, a system which involved close checking would be inappropriate in the new situation where the worker was to be given more responsibility.

Under the new payment system, each operative was allocated

to one of eight payment grades. The grades had been reached after considerable consultation during which specifications for the new jobs had been drawn up and interviews had been held with representatives of each grade in order to estimate the skill and responsibility involved. As a result of the new grading, the average increase in pay was around £3 per week. Only a very small number had increases of less than £2.

What then were the effects of the agreement—of the involvement discussions, the abolition of the bonus scheme, and the substantial decrease in supervision and increased flexibility of work tasks?

Chapter 4

THE CONTEXT OF WORK

We will begin by looking at those factors surrounding the job which Herzberg describes as 'hygiene factors' or 'contextual factors'. It has been asserted that such factors have little potency to generate favourable attitudes towards a job. In other words, when working conditions, pay and supervision are seen to be inadequate they will give rise to dissatisfaction, but when they are considered fair or tolerable they do not engender positive or good feelings about the job; there is merely a lack of dissatisfaction. Although such factors may not contribute significantly to satisfaction, they are none the less important. High levels of dissatisfaction may contribute to absenteeism, and more seriously, to unrest and disputes. What then was the impact of the agreement on such contextual factors? But first we will examine aspects of the working environment which were not affected by the agreement, and which consitute the constant element in the work context both before and after the changes.

Physical Surroundings

The human organism can habituate to and tolerate surprisingly high noise levels. The visitor to a noisy factory is amazed that men can work for eight hours a day on a shop floor where one literally cannot hear oneself speak. Since the Hawthorne investigations, noise, heat, fumes and other physical conditions have generally been dismissed as being of relatively little importance in job satisfaction. But at least one more recent study[1] of operators producing movie film found that although productivity was not improved by noise reduction, fewer mistakes were made. However, whatever the effects on pro-

[1] D. E. Broadbent and E. A. J. Little, *Occupational Psychology*, Vol. 34, 1960, pp. 133-40.

ductivity and quality in any particular work situation, improvements in physical conditions are likely to generate more favourable attitudes towards management. And conversely, as we shall see, adverse conditions are likely to permeate attitudes on a variety of issues.

In our case, satisfaction with physical conditions varied significantly between the three main divisions of the factory. From the auxiliary area where dissatisfaction was negligible, through the spinning area where we met a few complaints (mainly of heat), we come to by far the most dissatisfied group, the drawtwist operatives. Here the spun filament is stretched, twisted and wound on to bobbins. The noise level in this section is very high, making normal conversation impossible. Nearly two-thirds of drawtwist operatives complained of the noise, and its effect on general health was mentioned several times.[2] One man complained that 'It shatters your nerves'. Others said:

'The noise gets you down a bit occasionally. When I get home I'm tense; it takes me a long time to unwind and I think the noise is a lot to do with it.'

'I get a headache sometimes and it gets very hot when you're loading cakes. It's not a good job as regarding your health. You suffer from headaches and boredom. A lot of chaps stick this job for the money; you wouldn't get it anywhere else on day-work.'

Of the 63 per cent who were not bothered by noise or heat, particularly those in the spinning and drawtwist areas, one got the impression in many instances that they were putting on a brave face over this. It was fairly common for a respondent to mention that, although he was troubled sometimes, on the whole, 'You get used to it' or 'You just don't take any notice of it'. The ability to tolerate an unpleasant environment is by no means equivalent to the satisfaction of the worker's need to avoid the discomfort. Adaptation is effective only up to a

[2] No significant relationship has been found between physical working conditions and mental health. A. Kornhauser, *Mental Health of the Industrial Worker* (1965).

point, and it has been ominously suggested that it is achieved, in part at least, only at the cost of a degree of deafness.

We will have more to say about the effects of noise in the next chapter when we come to consider job interest.

Shift Work

A recent study of shift working found that on various social, psychological and physical criteria, its consequences for the worker are on the whole injurious.[3] Moreover, the worker on rotating shifts is worse off than workers on fixed shifts. These findings are worth looking at in more detail.

Shift work creates particular difficulties for the worker in his family life. For example, it hinders contact with children, and upsets the establishment of stable routines and division of labour between husband and wife. Irregular working hours also interfere with social life and men on rotating shifts have fewer friends. Where shift work is felt to interfere seriously with his non-work life, by both worker and his wife, particularly by the wife, it can have damaging effects on the worker's self-esteem.

Rotating shift and night workers are more likely to feel fatigued much of the time. Moreover, they more frequently suffer from poor appetites and constipation. This is put down to interference with 'time-oriented body functions'. There is also evidence of a diminished resistance to disease, two-thirds of them reporting an excessive number of severe colds and headaches. There is even some evidence that shift work may be a causal factor in some stress diseases, such as ulcers and rheumatoid arthritis. One final point of interest is that complaints were just as frequent from longer serving workers, the implication being that habituation and adjustment does not come with length of time on shift work.

Among the nylon spinners, about equal proportions liked, disliked, or were indifferent, and again, the proportion who disliked was higher in the drawtwist area, though the reasons for this are problematic. For some, the dislike was so strong that they would leave if the financial sacrifice were not too great.

[3] P. E. Mott, *et. al.*, *Shift Work* (1965).

'You're getting paid to a certain extent for the inconvenience and the loss of social life. I don't know what a single man sticks it for. You never get used to it; you get fed up, miserable at times. . . . It stands to reason, you go where the money is obviously. If you could leave for a few pounds a week less on days, you'd go.'

It is generally the disruption of social life, eating and sleeping habits and so on, that is mentioned by those dissatisfied.

The 'neutral' category hides a fair amount of discontent. For example, some mention that their wives were unhappy about their working on shifts and, although they themselves are not bothered by it, their wives' discontent is likely to contribute to their feelings about the job. Or take the spinning operative who remarked that 'You get used to it, but if they offered me the same money for days I should do days'. Others single out particular shifts—mainly afternoons and nights—which they disliked.

Even among those who expressed a preference for shifts this is not always unqualified. One drawtwist operative liked shifts for the variety and change but added, 'The afternoon shift is tedious—that's the shift I'll leave on'. However, a few expounded at some length on the advantages of working shifts.

'You spend more time at home when your children are about. On days you used to go to work in the dark and come home at night in the winter; decorating or working in the garden were limited to week-ends. In the summer, we can get away to the seaside when there are less crowds about.'

Pay and Security

We have moved a long way since the early days of Taylorism when it was believed that discrete increments in pay could call forth corresponding quanta of effort. In some circumstances pay can provide an incentive to effort.[4] But there is a growing body of evidence that such circumstances are by no means easy to achieve and the current trend is away from piece-rates[5] and overtime as a means of motivating extra effort. The

[4] For a review of this very complex literature, see V. H. Vroom, *Work and Motivation* (1964).
[5] W. Brown, *Piece-work Abandoned* (1962).

stimulus of monetary incentives is apt to wear off.[6] But more seriously, incentive schemes all too often provide a challenge to devise ways of getting round them, often at the expense of both quality and quantity. The incentive scheme in operation before the agreement was no exception. It neither encouraged high output nor quality.

'The chaps who were not particularly conscientious about the job didn't bother anyway—they knew very well that even if they lost the odd points here and there their money wouldn't drop a terrific amount.'

'I think incentives induced more carelessness in some respects. They used to be out for the bonus and not bother about the quality. A lot of people I know for a fact were careless and didn't do the job properly.'

'You only had just enough time to do the job in the allotted time, and if you saw a damaged carton you were inclined to let it go. Now you would see to it because you don't lose time on it. You not only get more done this way but the quality's better. You were restricted before to a certain limit, and you weren't allowed to earn over a certain limit. So I think people did that amount and that was it.'

'There were a lot of ways round the incentive scheme. For example, you could get a real easy job to do and you'd work hard at it. You'd need a thousand bobbins to make your shift but you may get fifteen hundred bobbins, say. Well, you'd do them and have five hundred start for the next day.'

Others mentioned that it was a matter of hurrying up to get your quota done and then sitting back. And, finally, we have evidence of the scheme leading to conflict over the allocation of jobs:

'When you had individual bonus people were inclined to cut the other's throat for the bonus, sort of thing . . . there was bickering over who got the best bonus job'.

[6] W. F. Whyte, *Money and Motivation* (1955).

In short, our results lend support to previous research on monetary incentive schemes: they frequently give rise to malpractices and unanticipated consequences which are contrary to the hoped-for results.[7] As a result of the agreement, operatives were individually graded and paid an annual salary weekly according to grade. There was universal approval of the change, and the abolition of the 'bonus' scheme which, in most cases, involved deductions for faulty work.

'It was the poorest incentive scheme I could ever think of. You already had your money, and all they did was try and take it off you. An incentive to me is working to get more.'

We are not saying that pay is unimportant. Indeed, it was mentioned more than any other factor during the course of the interviews and was certainly one of the most important of all the contextual factors to the majority of those interviewed. To many workers, it seems, so long as the pay is satisfactory, dissatisfaction in other areas can be tolerated; they are being paid for the inconvenience of shifts, noise and boredom. And as we shall see later, another factor, interpersonal relationships with work-mates is also regarded as a compensation for dissatisfaction with both contextual and motivational factors. Like the car workers, these men are prepared to trade unpleasant work for more money.[8]

Table 4.1: *Satisfaction with pay*

	%
Satisfied	61·7
Satisfied—with reservations	15·0
Dissatisfied	20·0
Don't know	3·3
	100·0 ($N = 60$)

Most (61.7 per cent) were satisfied with the pay (Table 4.1) and among the 20 per cent who were dissatisfied, most mentioned shift-work:

[7] D. Roy, 'Efficiency and the Fix', *AJS*, LX, No. 3. For a summary of the extensive literature on such practices, see C. Argyris, *Integrating the Individual and the Organization* (1964).

[8] J. Goldthorpe, *et. al.*, *The Affluent Worker: Industrial Attitudes and Behaviour* (1968).

'I wouldn't argue about the basic wage but it's poor for the shift work. I feel the shift allowance is insufficient for the inconvenience you're put to.'

A bargain implies that both sides feel they have benefited from the transaction, but not necessarily equally. How did the operatives see the distribution of benefits? Most agreed that both sides had benefited, but over half thought the company had gained more than the workers (Table 4.2).

'The workers are going to get a few shillings out of it, but the management's profit will be fantastic.'

'We're not getting a lot out of it—it's a rise that was really due to us. Obviously the firm will get the best of the bargain.'

'The Company wouldn't bring in these changes unless they were going to benefit from it. You've got to fight tooth and nail for all you can get.'

'It'll benefit the firm all right. They're getting a lot more work done now and there are less men doing that work. The worker has benefited but he could easily benefit more and they could still be well in pocket.'

One-third, however, thought that the benefits had been shared equally:

'We've obviously benefited straight from the start with the extra money, but in a long-term policy the firm will obviously benefit considerably. But of course, if it's a question of keeping the factory running and producing nylon at competitive prices we shall all benefit.'

Such comments, of course, do not necessarily reflect the actual situation. But it is the way in which the bargain is perceived which will determine behaviour. What is particularly interesting is the much less favourable view held by those in the drawtwist area; 87 per cent of drawtwist workers, as opposed to 56 per cent of spinning and 28 per cent of auxiliary workers, consider that the Company are deriving most benefit. The percentages of those believing that the benefits are being shared equally are 13 per cent, 28 per cent and 56 per cent respectively. However, it should be noted that not all of the operatives who thought that the Company was getting the best of the bargain were irate about it, but accepted this as the expected outcome and seemed reasonably satisfied with their 'cut'.

Table 4.2 : *Operatives' views on who benefited from the agreement*

	%
Company only	3·3
Worker only	—
Both, but Company most	56·7
Both, but workers most	—
Both equally	30·0
Don't know	10·0
	100·0 ($N = 60$)

Such differences in attitude do not reflect actual differences in pay between the sections. Why then are there such differences? And on what evidence do operatives base their judgement? In the first place, they are in line with differences which surfaced when we explored other aspects of the job, especially the contextual factors we examine in this chapter. It could be argued that feelings of contentment or deprivation deriving from the work situation result in a generalized feeling which spills over and influences the perception of other aspects. This is confirmed if attitudes to the distribution of the benefits from the agreement are cross-tabulated with the numbers of contextual factors with which operatives are dissatisfied.[9] If we take those operatives who are dissatisfied with between 0–3 factors and those dissatisfied with 4 or more factors as two groups, the relation is set out in Table 4.3.

The drawtwisters are most dissatisfied about their work context and also hold the most cynical views about managerial motives. This body of workers experience a number of deprivations in work, like extreme noise and monotony, and a possible

[9] Attitudes towards seventeen contextual factors were investigated. Thirteen are discussed in this chapter.

explanation of their cynicism is that they give vent to their frustrations on the management whom they consider responsible. Moreover, the issue about the sharing of benefits is interpreted mainly in a financial sense, and the possibility is that the greater the deprivations the more sharply will attention be focused on pay as a compensation and stronger feelings will be generated that their 'slice of the cake' is not as large as it should be.

Table 4.3 : *The relation between conditions of work and the assessment of who benefits*

	No. of aspects with which dissatisfied			
	0–3 %		4–11 %	
Who benefits				
Company benefits most	15	48·0	21	91·0
Company and workers benefit equally	16	52·0	2	9·0
	31	100·0	23	100·0
	$(p = 0 \cdot 01)$			

At the other end of the scale, auxiliary operatives are much more contented with their lot and display more generous feelings about the Company's motives. Although their work is little, if any, more interesting than that of drawtwist operatives, one important difference is that they have a far less stressful work environment in that it is relatively quiet and the temperature is comfortable.

Job security seems to be a basic need of most workers. The background to any agreement involving reductions in manpower is the general sense of job security. It certainly has figured prominently in attitudes towards technical and organizational change. Since such change is usually associated by the industrial worker with increased mechanization and rationalization leading to a paring down of the workforce, it naturally serves to arouse fears of redundancy. Improvements in pay are unlikely to be attractive or acceptable if they involve large-scale redundancies. This company was in an area where there were few other large employers in the vicinity. Most of the operatives had worked in the factory for many years, and had already seen a change in the ownership of the company.

The problem of redundancy was tackled mainly by allowing the labour force to run down through natural wastage. An essential part of the bargain was that no one would be made redundant. This assurance was, of course, a necessary pre-requisite for the changes. Although, even at the time of interviewing, three months and more after the start of the process of implementing the changes, 43 per cent still had doubts about their security, the balance, weighted heavily by financial considerations, had swung in favour of the changes.

Table 4.4: *Job security*

	%
Yes—secure	56·6
Yes, but qualified	16·7
No	6·7
Don't know	20·0
	100·0 ($N = 60$)

Rather more than half felt their jobs to be secure, a sixth felt a measure of security, while a quarter had considerable doubts (Table 4.4). For example:

> 'Yes, but you never know what trade requirements are going to be. Economic changes, government changes, anything could put the mockers on it straight away. That applies to any job now.'

This sense of uncertainty is shown in the answers of the 20 per cent in the 'don't know' category:

> 'There's a lot of men going into the pool [of labour] and you don't know whether they want those men or if they're just playing around for time—or getting them bored stiff first to make their own minds up to leave. If you knew more about it, if they gave you more information, you might feel more secure. But they don't give you nothing at all.'

> 'They told us it was a secure job for years, then a bit ago we had some redundancy. Then I think everybody lost that

feeling of security in this job. They've got a lot of excess labour here now and it will be interesting to see what happens to them.'

Others go further and, drawing on past experience, interpret the current situation pessimistically. These are the few who reply definitely in the negative:

'A lot of people are worried; there are 30 or 40 training at the moment on this shift. When they've finished, what are they going to do? When they made 200 redundant before, the local paper got it before we did and that spoilt it for everybody.'

But there were two groups in particular, the craftsmen and the supervisors, for whom the changes had substantial implications. A major basis for security and pay differentials for craftsmen is job demarcation. Certain tasks are defined as craft jobs and can only be carried out by men with a craft ticket.[10] The agreement involved allowing non-craft grades to carry out tasks previously preserved only for craftsmen. And the consequences of surrendering hard-won positions was a cause for considerable concern.

'It's cutting down skill. There'll be no apprenticeships. With the increased development of the agreement less skill will be required. You'll give a particular job away in stages. For instance, if an operative is given the job of putting in three wires they'll say: "If he can put in three he can put in six—and do that job as well." If you're giving skill away you've got to be well-compensated. Once you give a job away it becomes a collective job.'

'We've got more responsibility than under the bonus system and standard methods—we decide how to do the

[10] Apprenticeship and subsequent craft status performs a major regulatory function for skilled trades. It is the basis for job security, preserving certain tasks for skilled men and for wage differentials. To preserve such bargaining levers, craft unions, like professional associations, restrict membership. By contrast, those occupations with no specific bargaining lever, follow strategies which rely on extensive and non-exclusive recruitment. See K. Liepmann, *Apprenticeship* (1960), A. Flanders, *The Fawley Productivity Agreements* (1964), pp. 213–20.

job and what to use. But there's not a clear definition of what is skilled and unskilled. It's a job to know what to do to protect our job from our mates. . . . We're only doing half as many jobs now as we were doing four years ago. We've got a lot of installation work now—putting in new machinery, but when that's finished—and it's not going to last for ever—I can see there'll be a surplus of fitters.'

Serving an apprenticeship and earning craft status give rise to expectations of higher pay and greater security. Indeed, the sacrifices involved in the many years of apprenticeship are undertaken with such advantages as their aim. It is not surprising to find that the erosion of differentials is strongly resented:

'I served an apprenticeship for five years, starting off at about £1 18s a week I think it was. I had to do some night work at the tech. which I hated, and couldn't afford to go out with my mates who were flashing their big wage packets around and riding about on motor bikes. It doesn't seem worth it when semi-skilled men are within £2 of us.'

It's not just pay, it's also a question of status. Pay is a symbol of status; it is an element in the different evaluations of occupations:

'Mates are getting £20 to £22 a week, fitters are getting around £24, and operatives in the process areas take home more than me. . . . I think we should be on grade 8, but they don't consider us good enough. I'd rather be getting £25 a week on grade 8 than £25 a week on grade 7.'

Similar feelings of insecurity were generated among supervisors. But these will be discussed in more detail in Chapter 6.

Participation and Control

Studies of industrial workers have documented the widespread feelings that they have little control over the day-to-day activities which make up their jobs. The assembly-line epitomizes the most extreme case, where the worker has lost almost

63

all control over the pace of work and over his mode of operation. It is the machine which dictates and the man is slave to the machine. The operative carries out relatively simple tasks, which are meaningless and monotonous. The 'assembly-line syndrome' is a cluster of attitudes of intense dislike for these features of the work. Although technology is the major factor which determines the degree of autonomy and skill in the job,[11] this study is testimony to the possibility of changes in the organization of work within the limits set by a specific technology. The preliminary discussions aimed at maximizing the involvement of the operatives in the planning and execution of the changes. In this section, we are primarily concerned with the attitudes towards participation and the impact of the changes in machinery for participation which accompanied the agreement.

From previous studies, we can expect participation to have significant consequences. As we saw in Chapter 2, the importance of participative leadership, as distinct from laissez-faire and authoritarian styles, is a major message of recent literature.[12] Compliance is achieved through active participation in the decision-making process. This can be contrasted with the use of sanctions, threats and punishments. In short, the strategy is to achieve willing compliance with organizational goals. Those who work in the organization become motivated from within rather than coerced from outside. Decisions are ones which they have had a share in making, and are in this sense 'their' decisions.

In the case which we are studying, the aim was to introduce Likert's group participative type of management in which there is a high level of group-participation in decision making, with high levels of communication. Emphasis was on participation at the grass roots, between the supervisor and the work group. Such participation is characterized by immediacy and relevance in that there is often more immediate translation of decisions into action, and discussion is concerned mainly with the affairs of the team. This may be contrasted with the usual

[11] See, for example, R. Blauner, *Alienation and Freedom: the Manual Worker in Industry* (1963), for detailed studies of a number of technologies.
[12] See especially, R. Likert, *New Patterns of Management* (1961); W. Brown, *Explorations in Management* (1960); A. Gouldner, *Patterns of Industrial Bureaucracy* (1955).

procedure of representative councils where the majority of the workers are divorced from the decision-making body, where a complaint may be dealt with (even if it gets that far) a long time after it was originally raised, and where issues may be so general as to have little or no relevance to the particular problems of individual groups of workers. Our operators have at least a more or less regular chance to air an opinion, to ask questions important to them, and to discuss and make suggestions about the organization of the socio-technical environment within which they spend so large a proportion of their day.

Before the agreement, there was considerable machinery for consultation, including a works council and a suggestions scheme. Nearly half considered that the opportunities for dealing with complaints and suggestions before the agreement had been adequate (Table 4.5).

Table 4.5: *Adequacy of facilities for suggestions/complaints before the agreement*

	%
Sufficient	45·0
Insufficient	48·3
Don't know	6·7
	100·0 ($N = 60$)

Of the twenty-seven (45 per cent) who considered that the opportunities were sufficient only one thought they were worse under the agreement, while a substantial number reported an improvement. Out of the twenty-nine (48 per cent) who considered the opportunities insufficient, twenty-two of them reported at least an improvement, while seven of them still thought they were definitely insufficient. Complaints about difficult communications generally concerned the charge hands and foremen, the former generally being regarded as the stumbling block: 'You could complain to the chargehand but you didn't know whether he told the foreman or not. Now we have access to the foreman and things get done more or less straight away.'

Although there had been a substantial improvement, there were still unsatisfactory features.

E

'You can get complaints over if you are determined enough but you can get all tied up. There's no-one you can go to and know that something will be done. It takes you a month of Sundays to get a new pair of scissors.'

'If you put in a small complaint then it normally gets dealt with pretty quick. But, if it's something they don't want the management to know about, then it never gets there. If any of our machines go wrong you've got a hell of a job to get a fitter down here.'

In addition to the special meetings called to introduce the agreement and regular monthly meetings, more frequent informal shop-floor discussions were an important element in the strategy of seeking increased involvement at all levels. It was intended that such meetings should include as many members of the team as were available. Thirty-nine per cent of supervisors estimated that they called such informal meetings once a week or more, on average, 33 per cent around once a month, and the remaining 28 per cent convened meetings irregularly.

When questioned about the direct purpose of the meetings, nearly all the eighteen supervisors interviewed saw in them a means of providing information and of involving the operators. Two mentioned that they usually turned into complaints sessions. The information provided was usually technical in nature—new processes, feedback about performance in the shape of conversion efficiency figures and the like—but the meetings also dealt with general questions about wages, taxation and so on. Again, the main aim was to maintain a high level of operative involvement, by keeping them informed and interested about any new technical changes, but more particularly by discussing work methods and organization in order to arrive at joint decisions to which everybody had contributed.

'It's usually things that are going wrong—conversion efficiency, amount of waste we're producing—to get the general situation of the process across to them. . . . You've got to keep the quality up and the only way you can do this is the feed-back of what's going wrong so they can improve on it.'

'Supervisory changes, company policy, team performance, quality of yarn. Now you can get 'em to one side and really involve them. Before it was just a question of trying to put a point of view over in a noisy area. Before, if you had a bit of a problem, something that was niggling them, it just went on and on until the thing blew up. Whereas now, you have them in and say, "fair enough, I've had my say, now let's have your say. . . . Have you got any criticism towards me—am I watching you too much, am I away from the bank too much?" It's not a bit of good trying to be a bit aloof from them; you've got to work together and you get the best results.'

'I wouldn't dream of doing anything without telling them beforehand. It makes them feel involved, part of the plant.'

'I've reorganized the team to give me a slightly better coverage in spin doff. We all got together and planned it out within the team, and I should think that at least 50 per cent of it was their idea.'

'It usually ends up with their moans about one thing and another, but I find them very useful; you can clear the air a bit instead of letting things ferment. They blow their head off when they get into these meetings and that's a big help— you know where you stand with them.'

All supervisors found the meetings useful, not only as vehicles for passing on necessary information and as opportunities for operatives to suggest possible improvements, but also, as several mentioned, as a chance to find out about and forestall in advance, any trouble—perhaps arising from unwarranted rumours and suspicions.

These new shop-floor discussions were also the subject of favourable comment from operatives:

'We get together every so often—the works councillor, the shop stewards, foremen, etc., and we have a talk; you put your points forward and they get passed on. The works councillor can bring these things up at the meeting with the big nobs. Before, you get together with the blokes and see what their moans are—they get dealt with faster that way.'

Criticisms from operatives focused mainly on the unrepresentativeness of the formal discussions, rather than dissatisfaction with communications in general.

'When they were discussing the agreement they always picked a few senior men, the blue-eyed boys, who didn't know one bank from another. Now they've got different committees but people on them don't discuss them much with members of the teams. You're still getting a certain amount of seniority working.'

'They said there would be different chaps from each group each month at shop-floor meetings so that they'd get a wider view of the job, but it seems to me as though it's the same chaps that are going each time.'

A suggestions scheme had been in operation before the introduction of the agreement. Most (58·3 per cent) operatives felt that this continued to serve a useful purpose (Table 4.6).

Table 4.6 : *Attitudes towards the suggestions scheme*

	%
In favour	58·3
In favour—with reservations	15·0
Against	11·7
Don't know	15·0
	100·0 ($N = 60$)

One operative who had received an award for a suggestion and was in favour of the scheme remarked:

'You can make suggestions at "ways and means" meetings once in a blue moon, but any suggestions with regard to improving efficiency you would put through the Suggestions Scheme—then you'd get more of a hearing.'

[13] Operatives were questioned only about the formal meetings, while supervisors were asked to comment on the informal meetings as well.

Another operative from the same area thought it was irrelevant since the agreement, but he was the only man to express this opinion:

'We don't use it now because we have these discussions and new ideas are brought out and we take them up from there.'

Another spinning operative who had ideas accepted qualified his approval echoing several other replies:

'A better explanation for why suggestions are turned down would be an improvement.'

Although dissatisfaction was not widespread it gave rise to some strong resentment where it was felt that a proposal had been unreasonably ignored:

'This is the only method of getting suggestions over to the management—we never have any other meetings. I put a good suggestion in to run suction doffing guns from one air-line running along the top. Nothing came of it—then they brought it in. They'll never get another suggestion out of me!'

The Works Council appeared to stir no strong feelings, either for or against. Nearly half thought it was useful (Table 4.7).

'They get the idea of the person on the shop floor to higher management, which is a good thing. I read the minutes but I haven't got a lot of interest in it.'

'You've got to have somebody you can take your moans and groans to. There's somebody there to represent you.'

Those who were critical expressed no great feeling either, on the whole. One complained of too little information being passed on by councillors to them, and another operative said:

'It's tied—they can only suggest, talk things over. They can't do any real action.'

The 31 per cent in the 'don't know' category simply had had little or nothing to do with the council and generally were not interested anyway.

Table 4.7 : *Attitudes towards the Works Council*

	%
Useful	46·7
Ineffective	21·7
Don't know	31·6
	100·0 ($N = 60$)

Supervision and communications

Even before the agreement, relations with supervisors appear to have been fairly good (Table 4.8). But the agreement had been accompanied by a significant improvement (Table 4.9). One component in this improvement was the increased frequency of contact. But perhaps more important was the marked change in the relationships between supervisors and operatives. The strategy of involving operatives in change required that they were consulted. Instead of being given orders issues were discussed. There was a shift from authority to participation. Both supervisors and operatives were perceptive and vocal on this crucial change.

'Before the agreement the foreman was one man in the office and almost regarded as God by most of the operatives. He came on the shop floor perhaps once or twice a shift, probably knew the names of all of them although he didn't address them as he went by—he might nod. But now we know every man jack, we know his family history and everything. You speak to them every time you pass them, virtually. Another thing that didn't used to happen—this is social-wise—very few foremen used to play skittles or darts or anything with operators. But this happens now.'

Such changes were mirrored too in the comments of operatives:

'At one time all the foreman used to do was sit in his office—he never had a clue what went on on the floor. Now they're out on the shop floor and responsible for everything that happens in their team. Before they wouldn't bother to speak to you, but now they realize they're not far off our level.'

'We're having more contact with supervision than we did before. If you go to the office door you don't hesitate—"shall I go in or not?"—you just go straight in. You feel part of the job more. If you make a mistake your attention is drawn to it but you don't get this bullying attitude—"you shouldn't have done this or you shouldn't have done that".'

Table 4.8: *Operative evaluation of supervisory relations before the agreement*

	%
Good	40·0
Fair	53·3
Poor	6·7
	100·0 ($N = 60$)

Table 4.9 : *Impact of the agreement on operative/supervisory relations*

	%
Better	31·7
Same	61·6
Worse	5·0
Don't know	1·7
	100·0 ($N = 60$)

One result of the reorganization was a more direct relation between supervisors and operatives with a resultant improvement in communications. Previously, the foremen had charge of upward of forty men with the aid of assistant foremen. The supervisory changes involved both reducing the amount of inspection and breaking down the supervisory structure into smaller groups, with each supervisor in charge of a team of fifteen to twenty operatives.

'You've got a smaller group of men. Before, you could have a bank of, say, sixty men, whereas now we've got a bank of sixteen men. If you take sixty men into a room and give them a talk you couldn't get over what you wanted to get over. Now, with fifteen or sixteen men, the sessions are much better.'

'The suspicion has gone and it's purely due to talking to people. We can get them out of the area and talk to them now in small groups. Well, this we could never do before; there just wasn't the time for it, and in any case, it wasn't our job.'

With the new scheme, too, the post of communications assistant foreman had been created, and had met with general approval. The major source of complaint now focused on the allegation that the Technical and Development Division failed to channel information through the communications foremen and provided only the bare minimum of instructions:

'We don't get a great deal of technical information at the moment about a particular development. All we get is a piece of paper saying, "please run so many doffs off", and that's it. They're beginning to get the message now and they're putting on the paper the reason for it so you can go up to an operator and say, "I want this done, this is what we hope to achieve from it". They're more interested because they can see there's a reason for it. And I think that with the amount of changes that are taking place one is going to have to be able to absorb technical information and probably take over some of the technical jobs.'

'Technical section tend to be a bit protective of their own little job—"technical section is just a little bit better than you chaps; we've got to look after this".'

Inter-shift communication of information relating to plant conditions, technical instructions and the like, were also a source of criticism by over half the sample of supervisors. As a result of changes introduced over the preceding ten months or so, half those interviewed considered that an improvement had taken place here, although, of course, room for improvement still exists. A main source of improvement was the allocation of one information (or 'action') folder for each team instead of there being one to be shared by several teams.

'Before the agreement we would finish on a Saturday at two o'clock and come in on Wednesday night—God knows what's happened in between. There was one folder and you were queuing up to see what had gone on since you left Saturday. Now each team has got its own folder and you don't have to wait for somebody else to read it. The information is just appertaining to your own team and the operative can read it as well and get it first hand.'

Team co-operation and operative relations

One of the most important sources of satisfaction of the desire for personal worth is the primary group, the people with whom we are in close face-to-face contact. Consequently, 'most people are highly motivated to behave in ways consistent with the goals and values of their work group in order to obtain recognition, support, security, and favourable reactions from this group'. It is only in work groups characterized by 'a high degree of group loyalty, effective interaction skills, and high performance goals', that a man will fully utilize his abilities.[14]

Satisfaction with social relationships within the plant do not, of course, necessarily improve motivation or lead to higher productivity. If the goals of the work group are to regulate output according to some agreed norm, then group solidarity functions to restrict output. But if efficient job perfomance requires teamwork and co-operation, then harmonious relations with team-mates are important. And in this job, teamwork *was* important.

We found, as in the case of the car workers at Luton,[15] that primary group relationships are valued for much the same reasons; they are an antidote to boredom, monotony and physical surroundings:

'It's the sort of place that would really put you round the bend, not seeing daylight and working shifts.'

'You get a monotonous job and it's good to have somebody to talk to. Without it you'd take more notice of the noise and heat and everything.'

But the results of the changes introduced by the agreement

[14] R. Likert, *op. cit.*   [15] J. Goldthorpe, *et. al.*, *op. cit.*, p. 49.

were more positive than this. There was a marked increase in co-operation, both between teams and, more generally, improved relationships within teams between team-mates. Over two-thirds of those interviewed thought that there had been an improvement in co-operation. Indeed, all but one of the sixteen who considered there to be little co-operation before the agreement reported more since.

Table 4.10 : *Co-operation between operatives*

Before the agreement	%
Much	16·7
Fair amount	50·0
Little	26·7
Don't know or not applicable	6·7
	100·0
After the agreement	
More	71·7
Same	20·0
Less	3·3
Don't know or not applicable	5·0
	100·0 (*N* = 60)

Some of the comments made illustrate what more co-operation means to the operative:

'If work came up to be done, if you could get somebody else to do it you would. It's completely the reverse now. It makes a far more satisfying job if you work with a team that are going to do their share, rather, than competing with each other to do as little as possible.'

'Before, there was a cynical "couldn't care less" attitude. Now inter-floor relationships are much better—we know the chaps upstairs and they know us.'

'Before, you had your own machines to look after; now a team has got twelve machines and they're all yours. We are a team now—we were more individuals before. If I walk past a machine and there's an end down I go and throw it down, whereas before you were liable to walk past. We work a hell of a lot better together now. It's more friendly.'

'It's one hundred per cent better now. If we have a traverse bar break now everybody's there, whereas before you had to go and look for people to help.'

This enthusiasm in the Spinning section was quite remarkable and the essence of it is probably best expressed in the comment that 'the team are all as one now'. Although two-thirds of the drawtwist operatives said there was more co-operation, they had little to add and what enthusiasm there was was very muted by comparison with spinning. However, one man had this to say:

'Before one was arguing with another over what they should do and what they shouldn't do, where now you've got a block load to do and you all muck in and get on with it.'

In fact, one or two drawtwist operatives were critical of being moved from bank to bank as opposed to staying with the same team:

'All the banks are being mucked about by having so many men off and so many men on every day, and it's beginning to get a bit of a bind. And, of course, seniority's going to enter into this.'

But although there seemed less enthusiasm among the drawtwist operatives, a supervisor in this section reported a marked improvement in the co-operation within teams:

'It's very good, excellent . . . in my group they do all sorts of movements which they never thought of doing before. You'll get the four-man unit break off into pairs and pick up two machines, two men on each. If a certain job comes up—cake changing—over a job which hasn't got any cakes to change it's three times as long and you'll get two teams going together. And halfway through that you'll get two of them go away to start something else. I couldn't tell you at the moment who's working with who or what pattern they're working to.'

Similar evidence came from supervisors in spinning:

'We find that the team either side of you are quite co-operative. . . . We had a classic example of this about a month ago. We had a machine stoppage at half-past nine at night, there's a fair amount of work involved in this with twenty-four packs to change. So what do we get? We find at half-past nine it was embarrassing really to see the amount of men around the machine. Now they do this themselves; if I'm not about they'll just go into the teams themselves and do a doff for them.'

'The men will go to any team on the floor and say to the foreman, "Can we borrow a couple of your chaps for half an hour?" Before we couldn't do this because we were tied down with the incentive scheme. . . . They would help but pretty grudgingly. But under this new scheme they take it as a matter of fact; they're only too willing to do it.'

Some of the improvement in co-operation was directly traceable to the abolition of the bonus. In the auxiliary areas, for example, the necessity for some operatives to fulfil individual quotas in order to earn their bonus had given little scope for co-operation. Now, with the disappearance of the incentive bonus, co-operation has increased:

'If one man overlooks something now, another will pick it up and help him out or correct him if he's doing something wrong. You help each other because you think "Well, he'd do the same for me". Before, you had your quota to keep to and you hadn't got time to bother about anybody else.'

An operative in another section had similarly commented:

'When you had individual bonus people were inclined to cut the other's throat for the bonus, sort of thing. People seem to muck in better now. Before, there was bickering over who got the best bonus job.'

Not only had the agreement resulted in a marked improve-ment in co-operation, but also in the interpersonal relationships between members of teams. Most operatives attached considerable importance to having friends at work.[16] (Table 4.11.)

Table 4.11 : *Importance of having friends at work*

	%
Important	83·3
Neutral	8·3
Unimportant	1·7
Don't know or not applicable	6·7
	100·0 ($N = 60$)

Table 4.12 : *Relations with team-mates*

Before the agreement	%
Good	30·0
Fair	66·6
Poor	1·7
Not applicable	1·7
	100·0
After the agreement	
Better	26·7
Same	66·6
Worse	5·0
Not applicable	1·7
	100·0 ($N = 60$)

Table 4.13: *Satisfaction with the firm as employer*

	%
Satisfactory	70·0
Satisfactory, but qualified	20·0
Unsatisfactory	10·0
	100·0 ($N = 60$)

Attitudes towards firm as employer

As other studies have shown, workers may dislike, perhaps intensely, many features of the jobs, especially the boredom,

[16] By contrast, the workers at Luton attached little importance to this, although our sample, like the Luton men, were primarily instrumental in their orientation to work. *Ibid.*

monotony and pace of work on the assembly-line, yet have a favourable attitude towards the firm itself as an employer. Satisfaction here was high, focusing especially in fringe benefits, particularly sickness and pension schemes (Table 4.13).

Most dissatisfaction centred around the feeling that higher management was remote:

> 'I wish management would come in and talk to us like we were ordinary men instead of schoolboys, because you are treated like that sometimes. It would give them an interest in you and you in them, but they won't. They walk past you with their nose in the air. It's as if they don't want to know you're here; they're just not interested.'

Some base their resentment on particular incidents, as in the case of this particularly interesting observation:

> 'When this job was going well, after the agreement they had all the foremen and chargehands and union representatives, etc., and gave them a nosh-up for bringing in the agreement. Who brought it in? We did! I think it was one of the daftest tricks they ever pulled. It didn't half go down well with some of the blokes! I should say they accumulated more enemies over that than they ever had before. If they'd done it for everybody you'd have had a better bunch of men in here.'

Conclusions and discussion

Our evidence does not really lend support for the view that changes in the context of work (as distinct from the job itself) are of relatively little importance. Indeed, noise, heat and shift work were major sources of complaint tolerated by many only because pay was high. Moreover, dissatisfaction with conditions spilled over into more generalized attitudes towards company management.

Little could be done about such factors, at least in the short run, but where changes were possible, in methods of payment and supervision, there are strong grounds for believing that the effects went beyond reducing dissatisfactions and resulted in increased productivity by creating a situation in which there were no dis-incentives to attaining high levels of output and quality. Here, of course, we must stress the part played by the constant efforts to 'educate' operatives to the importance of quality so that quality-consciousness became part of the ethos of the job.

Most important, perhaps, were the changes in supervision with the introduction of shop-floor participation. The improvements in teamwork, co-operation and communications have been documented. Equally important, and more difficult to document, are the more subtle changes in attitude, involvement and motivation. The involvement discussions in some cases stimulated such enthusiastic proposals for job enlargement that supervisors felt it necessary to try to soft-pedal and to focus on more realistic goals. There is little doubt, too, that knowledge and experience were tapped that had previously lain dormant. As one supervisor said: 'It was fantastic the constructive suggestions, the constructive criticism about the way the place was running at the moment.' Not only were group decisions more fully accepted ('Once they'd agreed to something it was in, no question about it'), but there was a stronger motivation to see that they succeeded.

In short, participation does more than provide a therapeutic outlet for grievances, important as this may be. There was certainly a reduction in the number of grievances reaching higher managerial levels, 70 per cent being settled on the shop floor. It is also a source of positive satisfaction: '. . . being forced to do something is degrading, and hence one is both motivated to do something through fear, and motivated not to do it through pride'.[17] There is more likelihood that people will assume responsibility for their own rather than other's decisions: '. . . so long as supervisors set goals and make decisions they behave as responsible individuals and often cannot understand why their employees fail to accept a similar responsibility'. Groups are united with a common aim if they make the decision themselves, and as a result team spirit is high. There is more mutual help as a group responsibility is assumed.

Such gains in co-operation and teamwork should not, however, be interpreted as indicating a radical change in

[17] N. R. F. Maier, *Principles of Human Relations* (1952).

industrial relations. In particular, labelling operatives as 'salaried' does not automatically carry with it any fundamental change in attitudes towards the firm in the direction of any increase in identification with the interests of the firm, more commonly found among salaried workers. Most, as we shall see in Chapter 7, went into the agreement for the money. And a large proportion, indeed the majority in drawtwist, thought that the company had benefited most from the agreement. In short, it is perfectly possible for an increase in teamwork and co-operation on the job to exist side by side with a tough attitude towards the effort-bargain, and even considerable dissatisfaction with the equity of pay. But we will return to such broader issues in the final chapter.

Of course, participation is not an easily applied formula with guaranteed results.[18] It depends for its success on a number of conditions, not least the appropriate managerial ideology (e.g. a confidence in their workers' ability) and an employee-centred supervision. But it has been shown, and our evidence tends to support it, that given the right conditions workers will respond eagerly to the chance to exercise control over their working environment in organizationally useful ways as opposed to the usual strategies of independence in the form of restrictive practices and strikes.

[18] See D. McGregor, *The Human Side of Enterprise* (1960), Chapter 9.

Chapter 5

THE JOB CONTENT

As we explained in Chapter 2, the findings and theories of behavioural and social scientists were a big influence on the thinking of senior management and on the kinds of changes which it was planned to introduce. In particular, Herzberg's ideas on the ways in which the job itself can be changed to permit a greater degree of intrinsic interest and opportunities for self-actualization were most influential. It is such rewards as recognition, self-esteem and the enjoyment of the work itself which give rise to positive feelings about work. Men go to work for money, but they are motivated to work well by the satisfactions they gain from the work itself. And it was this aspect of the changes, providing opportunities for greater responsibilities and for more interesting work, to which management had attached particular importance.

The main determinant of the tasks which the worker carries out is, of course, the technology. And the rationale behind much modern technology is the view that the highest degree of efficiency can be achieved by breaking down complex tasks into relatively simple components which can be quickly learned. The limiting case is the assembly line in which the skill required is minimal, and jobs are simple and repetitive and the operative is highly constrained by the machinery on which he works. The consequence is a high level of monotony and fatigue.[1]

But the problems are not simply derived from the technology. Organizations are devices for allocating tasks to a large number of individuals and co-ordinating their individual efforts. Their characteristic feature is that some individuals tell

[1] Many studies have depicted the consequences—particularly in the car industry—of fractionized, repetitive work. See, for instance, C. R. Walker and R. Guest, *The Man on the Assembly Line* (1952); E. Chinoy, *Automobile Workers and the American Dream* (1955); R. Blauner, *op. cit.* (1964).

others what to do. Indeed, Argyris[2] goes so far as to argue that the requirements of a formal organization may be incongruent with the needs of mentally healthy people. In fact, infants are better suited to some organizations, since operatives are required passively to carry out instructions and are given little or no say in determining their own activities. Nor are they encouraged to improve their skills.

The jobs in the various sections of the factory which we are considering had many of these characteristics. The work was relatively routine and repetitive. But—and this is most important—some of the constraints on the exercise of autonomy and initiative flowed from the organization of the relations between men and machines rather than from the technology itself. And it is these which were capable of change, and to which management directed attention. These were the constraints of the rule book and of close supervision, epitomized by the following comments:

'The work before was very boring, very routine, very monotonous.'

'Before, you couldn't make any decisions whatsoever—you were just tied to what somebody else said. . . . You were like a puppet; you had to do everything you was told. . . . If you're partly running the job yourself you've got interest in it.'

It is not surprising that 83 per cent of those interviewed reported that there was no opportunity for making decisions on the job, and that 80 per cent felt the job to be monotonous—nearly one-third finding the work very monotonous (Table 5.1).

We turn now to look in more detail at various aspects of the work itself, and of the changes brought about by the agreement.

Job Interest

In view of what has been said about the technology and organization before the agreement, it is perhaps hardly

---

[2] C. Argyris, *Personality and Organization* (1957), Chapters 2 and 3.

surprising that the great majority of operatives found their work monotonous and boring.

Table 5.1: *Pre-agreement interest in job*

	%
Very monotonous	31·7
Fairly monotonous	48·3
Not monotonous	20·0
	100·0 (*N* = 60)

This was felt intensely by many operatives and was attributed to the repetitive performance of a limited number of standardized tasks, aggravated by periods of enforced idleness and clock-watching.

'Before, you felt you were in a rut—the daily grind; the same thing over and over again.'

'The work before the agreement was very boring, very routine, very monotonous.'

'It got you down, it got you right down. You came into the same job week after week, month after month, year after year.'

An acute awareness of the passing of time was a poignant element in the experience of many operatives:

'It was pretty monotonous—the same thing over and over again. You were watching the clock all the time before, working to time, and the time dragged. It's not that much more interesting now and yet the time seems to go a lot quicker.'

Table 5.2 : *Effect of agreement on interest*

	%
Much more interesting	11·7
More interesting	50·0
Little more interesting	18·3
No more interesting	20·0
	100·0 (*N* = 60)

The changes had made the work more interesting for most (80 per cent—Table 5.2), particularly for spinning, but less so for drawtwist. And for most, it was a decrease in *boredom* from having too little to do, rather than any decline in *monotony*, if we define this to mean the psychological feeling state resulting from repetitive performance of a limited variety of standardized tasks.

'Sometimes it was very, very boring. You could have two hundred unscheduled minutes, and any time the foreman could tell you to do this and that. Now, once you are out nobody will say do this or that because you are occupied all the time. Time goes by a lot quicker. Before you never had a rest room, and we used to lose ourselves, walk into another department. It was a waste of time. And then you'd bump into a foreman. You was out of place.'

There had been some element of job enlargement and this had contributed to some increase in interest, but the job remained essentially monotonous. Job enlargement, in the sense of increasing the number of tasks performed but without raising the level of skill required, does little to eradicate monotony. 'A worker goes from one repetitive rhythm to an equally monotonous one; the diversion has only lasted for the few minutes required to get used to the new rhythm.'[3]

'You've got a variety of jobs to make a break from the actual doffing now, but it's not interesting to the point that you can enjoy it.'

'Before the agreement there was not the slightest interest for its own sake; it was just like a production line. Doffing is just doffing—in and out of the boxes. They said that under the agreement you wouldn't get so bored, but I think the basic principle's there still; it's a boring job. In the beginning the interest was there because you were doing a bit of something different but there was nothing really different. The main job was to doff the machine. After all, that's all the management wants is to get the machines doffed and running again.'

[3] A. Touraine, *Workers' Attitudes to Technical Change* (1965).

84

Another feature of the work organization which aggravated the boredom was the hated patrolling. Each operator had a two-hour stint patrolling the machines looking for faults—breakages, wrong string-ups, wrong pack usage, and so on. In fact, little was ever found out of place and the task was regarded as the most painfully tedious of them all.

Meaning of Work

The rewards which work can offer derive in part from the satisfaction in seeing the contribution which the worker makes to the total product. The meaning of work depends on the worker's relationship to the process, to the organization of work, and to the product.[4] There is little meaning or creative satisfaction from a fractionized job in which the contribution of the individual worker is small and repetitive.

Operatives were first asked whether they had at least a fair idea of the total manufacturing process, that is, what happens to the yarn before it reaches their section and after it leaves them. Not surprisingly, every operative reported a knowledge of the various stages of production which they gained during their induction period, through job appreciation sessions, and through occasionally working in other areas. In view of the job enlargement resulting from the agreement it was hypothesized that the work would be more meaningful for some operatives but particularly those in the spinning area. However, only 10 per cent of the sample said they had a better idea of their job and where it fitted in with the rest of the factory. Five of these were spinning operatives of whom one elaborated his answer as follows:

'You get a far wider knowledge of the job now. In the spinning area your job covers from the unit floor, through extrusion, spin doff, right through to the denier board. Of course, by learning all these jobs you appreciate your original job more. It all fits into little slots now.'

Ninety per cent of operatives did not feel the changes were so great as to make much difference to their wider job knowledge and appreciation, drawtwist people pointing out that,

[4] R. Blauner, *op. cit.* (1964).

after all, they still worked in the one area. Many spinning operatives reported that they, too, were mainly confined to one floor, and one operative had worked solely in the pack room since the introduction of the agreement over three months previously. Thus, although operatives were by no means ignorant of the total process, the agreement had done little to widen the scope of their activities and enhance their sense of purpose in the job.

This question of contextual job knowledge recurred unexpectedly in response to questioning about creativity in the work. Respondents were asked whether their job gave them a feeling of satisfaction out of having made or created something for themselves, seeing an end-product with which they can identify and which means something to them. The replies were overwhelmingly in the negative with 88 per cent remarking that it is not that kind of work.

> 'I don't think there's anything that would make you proud. You couldn't say, "Well, I've done that", you just pack a box of yarn, and you've packed thousands of boxes of yarn before. The machine makes the bobbins whether your back is turned or not. A man that is doing a job that he's proud of, that he's good at—he's going to do a better job. His mind is going to be more at ease.'

> 'You never see an end-product. I mean, what is a bobbin? It looks just like a milk bottle.'

However, one might have expected that the majority of workers, habituated to intrinsically unrewarding work, would not be particularly bothered by this aspect. Yet, when asked whether they considered it important in a job to see an end-product in this way, 72 per cent replied in the affirmative.

> 'I've often wished they would take us to some of these factories, even if it was only on our days off, to see some of the raw product made up. You might get a bit of satisfaction out of knowing what you're doing and what it leads up to and what it requires to keep up to the standard.'

As we shall see, this was a facet of work that gave rise to a great deal of comment, and one sensed in many cases that an important element of work satisfaction was under discussion. Among those who did not experience a need for meaning and creativity in the job one remarked that:

> 'You get into a frame of mind up here where you're not actually concerned so much with an end-product but more with keeping the machines running and producing grade 1 yarn.'

Others in this category said they had become resigned to this feature of the job now; as one operative put it, 'I suppose I've been here too long and I just accept these things'.

On the other side of the coin, the ensuing remarks demonstrate the intensity of feeling of many operatives on this point:

> 'You never see the finished product. We're spinning yarn out there now but you never see where it finishes up or what it finishes up as. You just see the filaments go down the chimney and that's it.'

A former coal-miner expressed his frustration in this way:

> 'As a miner you were paid for output, for the amount of coal you shifted, but here you don't know how much you're making. Five million pounds of yarn in the warehouse doesn't mean anything to me—it doesn't tell me how much I'm making.'

A spinning operative also relates his past work experience in this instance as a skilled fitter, to the nature of his present job:

> 'When I worked at . . . we used to get our parts from the stores and within three days you'd have a completed engine. We could see an engine growing, and you have a certain amount of satisfaction from seeing what you've done. Whereas here, you do a part of a job and that's it, you never see anything further of it.'

Work in the drawtwist area is no more meaningful for the operative, as this comment demonstrates:

'We don't see anything in this job. You'd get more interest in a job by knowing what you're doing it for. As far as I'm concerned, I'm just putting up nylon, I'm drawing it and putting it into a box. That's it—it doesn't mean anything at all to me. The only thing that's keeping me here at the moment is the money. If I knew more about the job from the start to the finish then I'd be a bit less concerned with the money.'

This is a particularly interesting comment for it illustrates an attitude common to most of our sample, namely that where intrinsic rewards are absent, extrinsic rewards are increasingly sought after. As we saw when we examined contextual factors such as physical working conditions and shift working, financial reward and the standard of living it affords are seen as compensation and the chief reason for coming to work. This drawtwist operative finds other compensation for the lack of creativity:

'It's more satisfying to have something you've done yourself and it's all part of you. Our only satisfaction is that we work as a team. This is what's rewarding.'

Finally, the comments of this drawtwist supervisor are worth quoting for the light they shed on the difficulties of the foreman in this type of technology and the unexpected confirmation of the feelings of meaninglessness in the work which many operators expressed. It also raises the question as to how far, in spite of the co-operation of the supervisors, a human relations approach will pay dividends in the face of hostile technological factors militating against worker involvement and interest:

'I try to broaden their knowledge of the whole job. But you've got a direct conflict between the job and trying to instil interest in operatives to do the job better . . . I couldn't quite see anything new in the agreement. In the factory I was in before we used to have a hundred men—it was carpentry and joinery—and we had no work study and times to do the job or anything like that. The blokes used to get stuck in and get on with it. But that job was more interesting mainly because—and this is the biggest bug-bear in this plant—you saw the end-product. This is one of the underlying things all the time down there—this sense of frustration in not being able to achieve anything. Everybody wants an incentive to work, and pride in one's job is a big factor—how well you do the job. And to get this pride you need something to look at.'

Although these operatives are alike in that they find the work itself largely meaningless, they fall into two groups, the dividing line between which is by no means clear cut. On the one hand, there are those who miss the opportunity for creative self-expression in their work and react unfavourably to a machine process that turns out a standard, impersonal product. They can have little conception of their individual output, let alone decide the techniques for making the product or affect its character in any way that would put their personal stamp on it. The coal-miner needs to see what he, as an individual, has produced; total production figures tell him nothing about how well he is performing his job. The fitter used to derive some satisfaction out of contributing to the completion of an engine; but here he is concerned with a part of the process which does not visibly change the product at all, and then he sees nothing further of it. And another is unable to take a pride in a job that churns out a homogeneous product with which he cannot identify because 'the machine makes the bobbins whether your back is turned or not'.

On the other hand, there are those making up the larger group who, although they have at least an outline knowledge of the total process and the function that their job serves within it, find this insufficient to give their work any intrinsic meaning. For, after all, the end product is only a bobbin from which recognizable products are made only after it leaves the factory. The process or chain of manufacture is truncated, left in mid air so to speak, as far as our operatives are concerned. Hence the fairly frequent suggestion, as we have already mentioned, that tours of factories which continue the process— knitters and weavers for example—would give the job interest, put it more in context.

Responsibility

Inevitably, a machine-minding technology gives little scope for the initiative of the worker. And where his movements are further circumscribed by a set of rigid job procedures, such a worker is likely to feel powerless, impotent,[5] and other-directed. His pace of work and his every action are determined by others, by supervisors, and by those who designed the machine. This is in part a consequence of the technology, but more importantly of a managerial ideology which sees the worker as passive, lazy, and requiring strong discipline to prevent him straying from the path of standard procedure.[6] A supervisor remarked that before the agreement his job was to enforce a work organization that turned the men into 'clockwork doffers'.

A growing volume of social science literature[7] suggests, however, that where it exists, such passivity has been instilled by the very practices which assume it to be characteristic.[8] Organizations which deny the possibility of responsibility and initiative generate the very qualities which they are designed to regulate. If this view is correct, then to call forth responsibility and initiative requires positive policies to promote opportunities for the exercise of responsibility.

This agreement marks a significant change in management thinking. The workers were given more control over the organization of their work schedules, certain inspectional and checking duties and responsibility for liaising with other departments over matters such as material supplies. Concomitantly, there was a reduction in work checking by quality patrollers and a decrease in production-oriented supervision.

The transference of responsibility on to the shoulders of the operative is one of the most significant features of the agreement, the intention being to satisfy assumed needs for the exercise of autonomy and self-actualization in work. How much say and self-direction have workers as a result of the agreement? Are there any blocks to their exercise of respon-

[5] See R. Blauner, *op. cit.*, for a comparative account of powerlessness in four technologies.

[6] McGregor, *op. cit.*

[7] See, for example, A. Turner in *Man and Automation* (1956), and C. Argyris, *Integrating the Individual and the Organization* (1964).

[8] An example of a 'self-fulfilling prophecy'.

sibility? And from their experience so far, what would be the operatives' reaction to more?

As a first step in understanding operatives' attitudes towards responsibility, we tried to find out what they thought were the intentions behind the scheme. Did they interpret it cynically as another move to get more work out of them, or was it regarded as a *bona fide* attempt to place more trust in them on the part of management? Although some cynicism was met with, 80 per cent of those interviewed saw it as a sign of more trust, remarking that 'it makes an operator feel that it's more worthwhile', and that it is 'going to instil more trust in both sides—you sort of get to know each other that much better'. The sizeable minority who were dubious or cynical about the responsibility proferred the following opinions:

> 'I see it as a sign of getting more for paying less. It's ICI's saviour.'

> 'Outward appearances would suggest more trust but in fact they've got a better check on what's being done now because you've got a record to keep and you virtually sign for, accept responsibility for, a machine, so that if anything goes wrong they've got a record of who did it.'

Before the agreement, few (less than 17 per cent) thought they had any chance to exercise discretion or take decisions. The supervisor had always to be consulted before any actions to deal with exigencies, for example, could be taken. Those few who reported that there was scope for doing the job in their own way were usually talking about informal behaviour which was not sanctioned by the organization. You 'cut corners' only when the foreman's back was turned, and you were always 'looking over your shoulder'.

> 'Standard methods are all very well, but when you've got a rush on you're liable to cut corners. On the fork-lift I could lift up half a dozen buggies and get them from here to there in the time it takes me to do three by standard methods.'

As a result of the changes, most (80 per cent) thought there was more opportunity to take decisions, and most (88 per cent) thought there was less supervision. Again, most (82 per cent) thought they had more responsibility now than before the agreement (Table 5.3).

Table 5.3 : *Effect of the agreement on responsibility*

	%
Far more responsibility	11·7
More responsibility	65·0
A little more responsibility	15·0
No more responsibility	8·3
	100·0 ($N = 60$)

'We order our own boxes, bags, etc. No matter what job it is you do it yourself to get your job going. We are never waiting for anything. Instead of asking shall I do this? or is it all right to do that? you do it yourself—because we could always see that it wanted doing.'

'If anything went wrong in the area you reported it and just sat back and waited for the result. Where now you've got the interest there to go and look to it yourself and you feel as though you've done something.'

However, to some the changes were not seen as making any significant contribution to increased responsibility:

'If you call inspecting bobbins more responsible, well that's the only little bit we have. Before, we just used to cut the waste off and put them in boxes, now we inspect them. It's too little to make any difference. . . . If anything crops up you've got to see the foreman. One's got to be careful about taking things on.'

Generally speaking, the changes have not only been accepted as increasing responsibility, but have been welcomed by most (83 per cent). Some regard it as a vehicle of self-realization, the means to personal growth in work. They feel that the changes have marked the end of personal stagnation whereby workers react to orders 'like puppets' as opposed to doing their own thinking and organization; there is a consequent feeling of having 'achieved something' and 'It gives you a bit more confidence in yourself'. 'You are treated as adults—as responsible adults'. On the other hand, of those operatives who consider they have, in fact, got more responsibility there are some (a minority) who are not interested anyway:

> 'We get paid for it and we're here to do a job of work. It doesn't matter to me.'

These conclusions are reinforced by the observations of the supervisors, eleven of whom considered that over three-quarters of their operatives had assumed added responsibilities, and six thought that this was true of between 50 and 75 per cent. The general opinion is that whereas most workers have shouldered their obligations to plan work, check machinery, and so on, an apathetic or unco-operative minority have not.

> 'It's just the awkward ones in the team who still say, "I don't think I should have to check machines anyway", or "I'm quite happy doffing, I don't want to do that". With some of the old type who've left school a long time ago they are afraid. And you've got the young chap who's capable of doing the job but he doesn't want to know.'

One supervisor commented that although his team are willing to carry out tests involving responsibility, he finds that there is a conspicuous lack of initiative. He also mentions the development of informal sources of authority arising within the team and militating against the assumption of responsibility by the whole team:

> 'I could quite confidently give my men another job aspect to do and know that they'd do it. But the thing that I can't get 95 per cent of them to do is to do this without being told to do it. . . . You've got to go along and ask them; then they'll do it. . . . One danger that is creeping in is that you've got, in every group, two or three men with strong personalities. Now these two or three men decide which job will be done next or how much work will be done. So what

93

you've got is a substitution of the supervisor. There's no point in substituting one for another.'

How far this is idiosyncratic to this team we cannot say. Further researches might well explore how far the devolution of formal authority generates a tendency for a structure of informal authority to develop.

Although the majority of operatives had welcomed and accepted the added responsibility (with varying degrees of enthusiasm and for various reasons), opinions were more divided on the desirability of further extensions along these lines. Indeed, only a third welcomed the idea of still further responsibility (Table 5.4). And of these, many considered that it should be accompanied by more pay. Relatively few wanted more responsibility for its own sake.

Table 5.4 : *Attitudes towards further extensions of responsibility*

	%
In favour of more responsibility	35·0
Not in favour or indifferent	38·3
Unsure	10·0
Not possible	16·7
	100·0 (N = 60)

The large proportion of almost a half of the sample who were not in favour or unsure about more responsibility is rather surprising in view of the fact that 83 per cent of the sample are in favour of their present responsibility. It could be, of course, that workers' aspirations have been met—albeit perhaps only temporarily. McGregor put forward the idea that a worker learns his passivity through his experience in bureaucratic organizations and maintains that he will discover his potential or desire for autonomy and responsibility when opportunities are given. It is possible that the scope of responsibility is too narrow to overcome the indifference of many workers. A more optimistic interpretation of the data is that a radical attitudinal change such as is being attempted here is not likely to meet with overnight success but must be regarded as a long-term process. One must remember in this connection that the changes were only two and a half months old when the interviews started. However, this is a theme to which we will return.

One final index of operatives' attitudes towards responsibility is their perception of the future role of the supervisor. Most thought that fewer would be needed in the future. But only 5 per cent thought that supervisors could be dispensed with completely.

> 'They just go round now and see that you've got it right. Once we can get the teams organized properly and get the right kind of co-operation in the team I don't think they'll be needed as much.'

> 'They make sure everything's going all right with you. We don't really need them to be quite honest—we could do it ourselves. In future they'll become a thing of the past. They'll trust you to get on with the job, and that's it.'

Most who considered that he is, and will be needed, mentioned 'paper-work' (checking-in, booking lieu days and holidays, keeping records), checking on quality, and a few mentioned sorting out team strengths, training, and maintaining the supply of work materials. Many thought that somebody was necessary in case of emergencies and to give advice should it be needed, but with regard to running the job most operatives considered him superfluous:

> 'If you've got a slacker in your team you do something about it yourself. . . . The responsibility is put more on to the men now. In other words, if you've got somebody who wants to sit around it's more likely the other chaps will say "get your finger out and get cracking" rather than they would before. . . . Having got his team trained to do any job I shouldn't think there's a heck of a lot for him to do. Most of his jobs have been handed over to the operator, and we've got a communications section. If there's a particular team overloaded or short of labour, it's the communications section that deals with that. I don't know what they will have to do in future—somebody may have an idea.'

'They're there if you've got something come up that you're not quite sure of—someone you can fall back on.'

'He will have very little to do. They'll have to have somebody to check people in. You need someone if drastic measures are necessary.'

Notwithstanding the important reservations we have already discussed about the strength and frequency of the need for more responsibility, we have evidence here of a current of feeling heading more or less in the direction of responsibility at work. There is still much caution and wariness of having the prop of supervision taken away altogether, but the general trend of opinion indicates that there is a reasonable chance that the agreement will be successful in its aim to reduce supervision. However, the emphasis must be on 'eventual', for how long an attitudinal change as radical as this will take is very much a subject for conjecture.

Use of abilities

As we have seen, an important element in recent theories of motivation is their emphasis on the declining importance of material and physiological needs. As our more basic needs for food, shelter and material possessions are satisfied, we become more aware of the need for personal growth, for the exercise of skills and abilities which are intrinsically rewarding. In the words of Maslow, 'A musician must make music, an artist must paint, a poet must write, if he is to be ultimately happy. What a man can be, he must be. This need we may call self-actualization.'[9]

As we saw in Chapter 2, such ideas have had considerable influence on the work of Herzberg and his associates. And whereas the need for food and shelter can be saturated, the satisfactions derived from personal growth are not satiated in this way. Hence the importance of self-actualization as a 'motivator'. The use of skills and abilities is itself rewarding. The creative artist does not need to be persuaded or cajoled into painting by the carrot of money or the stick of starvation. Indeed, he paints regardless, and although the romantic image

[9] Maslow, *Motivation and Personality* (1954).

of starvation in a garret is an exaggeration for many, it is true that money and material possessions are often secondary for the dedicated artist, scientist, politician, scholar, priest.

Spinning operatives are not dedicated. And, as we saw in the previous chapter, most are in the job mainly for the money. But as Herzberg points out, men go to work for the money, but they work well if they find the job itself rewarding. How far then did the jobs we are considering make use of the skills and talents of the operatives? Before the agreement, the answer is clear enough:

'We were treated almost as an idiot. You weren't paid to think.'

'You hadn't a chance to use any initiative or intelligence. No matter what went wrong you'd go to the chargehand and put it in his lap.'

Well over two-thirds thought that before the agreement the job did not make the best use of their abilities. Nearly half thought there had been an improvement (Table 5.5).

Table 5.5 : *Impact of the agreement on the use of skills and abilities*

Pre-agreement	%	
Abilities used	33·3	
Abilities not used	58·4	
Don't know	8·3	
	100·0	($N = 60$)
Post-agreement	%	
Better use of ability	46·6	
Same use of ability	48·4	
Worse use of ability	1·7	
Don't know	3·3	
	100·0	($N = 60$)

This most perceptive comment points to the damaging effects of fractionized jobs and their effect in retarding personal growth, self-confidence, and competence:

'Those men out there now will be on drawn yarn, the next week on undrawn, the week after on waste cutting, the next on scales. At first some of them protested that they couldn't use a scale. Men who have been six years stuck on one job are a bit frightened when you move them on to something else. There was one man who worked three years on nothing but pushing buggies; he was frightened to death to go cutting off waste. Now that he's on the machines he's as happy as a king. It's like opening up a new world entirely. He's not the only one. They've never realized they could work those machines and do that. They're finding themselves a different life entirely through working these machines. It's a good thing this agreement—changing people around. I see a change in most of the chaps in here in that way.'

However, we must not exaggerate the effects of the agreement. Some interpreted the better opportunities for the use of abilities to mean less hanging about and waste of time, although others saw it as giving greater scope for initiative: 'It allows a bloke the chance to do the job in his own way. We've all got our own ideas on how to do a job.' Only one-third thought that the job now required more skill than before. Even in the case of those who considered the job to be more skilled now, their supporting remarks betray little excitement and do not describe very sweeping changes: 'The technical aspect of the job requires you to be more accurate. You are required to remember a lot more.' Other operatives thought the job more skilled because they had taken over many of the chargehand's jobs such as machine checking, while another said that, because they are doing a few jobs that the fitter used to do, it's more semi-skilled labour now. However, the most typical remarks were: 'You're still doing the same job with little bits tacked on' and 'There's no skill in the job as far as I can see'.

A further index of the opportunities for personal growth is the extent to which operatives feel that they are 'getting on' and making progress in the job. About one-third felt that things were better after the agreement. Ten per cent mentioned that the chances of advancement to supervisor were less now. Typical comments from the 50 per cent who thought there was no difference were:

'Not apart from £4 a week extra—it's still boring.'

'You were standing still before the agreement and you aren't doing much different now. It's still basically the same.'

In the case of most of those interviewed this obviously wasn't a feature of working life to which they had given a lot of thought. Some people said they were not sure, or did not think about it. Even though improvements in job satisfaction in many respects have been reported, one sensed that unprompted by the question, few would have regarded such changes as 'progress'. The fact that workers accustomed to unsatisfying work are not in the habit of evaluating change in this way ought not to surprise us, for a working life devoted to seeking extrinsic rewards can hardly be expected to engender such lines of thought.

Recognition

Recognition of work well done is an important reward. It was not the original intention of the agreement to bring about any changes in feelings of recognition. And indeed, there is no evidence from the operatives themselves to suggest that any changes have resulted. None the less, in order to embrace as many factors as possible in the composite picture of job satisfaction, it is necessary to take account of this one which, as it turned out, was more important than one might have guessed.

Asked whether they considered it was important to receive praise or credit for good work, over two-thirds replied that it was. But nearly two-thirds reported that such praise or credit was not forthcoming. Those who considered praise unimportant typically commented: 'You're paid to do a job and do it correct', and 'I don't want somebody to come patting my back every time I do something good.'

However, this kind of attitude is not shared by the 68 per cent who attached importance to recognition, most of whom express their feelings on this matter in a way that leaves one in little doubt about the significance of this factor in job satisfaction and motivation. Very few interviewees reported instances of praise being given, one mentioning circulars from management, and another told of a foreman thanking them for 'unloading lorries right on home-time'. But these were isolated cases.

> 'You get the blame but never the praise. A bloke spotted a thing that I don't think a man on this floor would have spotted. There were two flows and it was only by a thousandth of an inch that you could tell the difference. One was a slightly thicker yarn than the other through a wrong pack. But he didn't get no praise.'

> 'It's taken for granted. We've passed remarks about that—the emphasis is on the bad workmanship and nothing is said when things go well.'

> 'If you do anything right you get nothing; if you do anything wrong you get a rollicking.'

Comments by those who consider praise important underline the high premium put on recognition and of the significance of this factor in the satisfaction of ego needs.

> 'If a bloke says to you "You've done a good job here", it makes a big difference, but if a bloke is going to jump on you every time you make a mistake, it hurts.'

> 'Recognition is extremely important. To give praise where it's due is a damn good thing—you give the man incentive.'

> 'I think it's very important. To some individuals a pat on the back is better than a few shillings in their pocket.'

> 'It makes you feel that you have achieved something. If the foreman were to say, "Well, thank you very much, you've done a good job there", you could see it was being appreciated.'

> 'If you do find something and you get a bit of recognition for it you feel ten feet tall.'

> 'I've always maintained that if you see a fellow doing a good day's work and you mention it, it does a lot for his morale. It's a thing I've always thought a lot of.'

In order to estimate the dissatisfaction associated with this factor, or at any rate the percentage of operatives who felt a need for recognition without it being satisfied, the incidence of praise given was correlated with the need for it. The result was that, out of the thirty-seven who received no recognition, twenty-four (or 40 per cent of the entire sample) considered it important to them. This is a sizeable proportion and a problem which will not become any more easily surmountable with a run-down of supervision should this be contemplated—although from the evidence we have just examined it appears that foremen do not consider verbal rewarding of industrious behaviour to be a very integral part of their supervisory role. One conceivable solution is that increased satisfaction of ego-needs in other spheres will compensate for lack of satisfaction here.

Fatigue

Finally, we come to a factor which is an index of the impact of work on the operative. Early studies in industrial psychology were much preoccupied with the causes of fatigue and sought to mitigate such factors as noise, heat and poor lighting, which were considered to be major contributory causes. Work study and ergonomics are also the outcome of the perspective which sees fatigue as a function of the expenditure of energy. More recent studies would stress the psychological component in fatigue. And our evidence underlines the importance of boredom, rather than physical factors.

Before the agreement, over two-thirds of the operatives reported fatigue (35 per cent often, 33 per cent sometimes). A variety of causes was put forward to explain this tiredness, among them being the heat, the noise, shift working, and in only a few cases was heavy work pointed to. Too fast a pace was never blamed; in fact, the opposite was most frequently cited, that is, the boredom of killing time between doffs, and so on. It is an interesting paradox that fatigue can be attributable both to the pressure of an over-fast work pace on the one hand and to a work organization which enforces lengthy periods of idleness on the other.

'The only thing that made you tired was the boredom. Sitting around waiting for something to do made you tired.'

'Not tired through hard work, but when you sit about so much you go home feeling really weary.'

'Boredom makes you tired. It's the most boring and tiring thing out to watch the clock.'

As we would expect from the effects on the level of boredom and monotony of the reorganization of work, the level of fatigue has dropped, with 33 per cent of operatives reporting an improvement. However, a third of the operatives who experienced fatigue report no change. Only 6·6 per cent of all operatives find the job more fatiguing now.

'You don't feel so tired now—you've got more to occupy your mind. The time's gone before you know it.'

Some recognized that they were less tired now, even though they were expending more physical energy:

'I think everybody's happier because you used to get a bit of hanging about before, and it used to get boring, and you'd get tired. You're learning more things now and you've got more interest. . . . Things are getting heavier—heavier bobbins, heavier cakes, and it's all go; you seem to use more energy. I think everybody would rather have it, mind; if you've got something to occupy your mind the time's gone in no time. Before, you were looking at your watch, worrying when to start your machine.'

However, for this operative who found the job very monotonous and tiring before the agreement the changes have done nothing to alleviate his dissatisfaction:

'I think I can put this under three headings; if I said boredom, shift work, and heat—you put those three together and I think you've got the whole problem solved. It makes you really tired.'

As in the case of boredom and monotony, fatigue has been reduced in part by more interesting work, but primarily by removing the periods of enforced inactivity which were the main cause of ennui. It is not so much, then, the monotony of the work which the agreement has ameliorated as the distressing symptoms of mental fatigue brought on by a lack of occupation.[10] This was exacerbated by an absence of rest-rooms, particularly in noisy areas. Thus, it appears that the reorganization has had the effect of decreasing fatigue and the dissatisfaction brought on by boredom by providing the opportunity to work throughout the shift without enforced or built-in intervals of inactivity.

Conclusions and Discussion

What then were the overall results of the organizational changes? Job enlargement plus less supervision had undoubtedly contributed to a marked decrease in boredom. And the work now made greater demands on abilities. But basically the work remained monotonous. Indeed, we were struck by the marked difference in enthusiasm and satisfaction for the work itself among the nylon spinners compared with workers in highly automated plants which we were studying at the same time.[11] Consequently, for most, work had little meaning. It was essentially a means to an end—a source of income. Although reorganization had brought about some improvement, neither the tasks nor the product provided much basis for satisfaction or were seen as in any sense meaningful. This lack of meaning is epitomized in the remark, '. . . what is a bobbin? It looks just like a milk bottle'. In short, however significant the gains from organizational changes, the technology in the last analysis set the limits to job enlargement. Whether these limits have yet been reached is another matter.

What these findings do support is the optimistic view that workers are capable of development, of accepting more responsibility, and of greater initiative. Even the very modest and short period of re-education and the small extensions of responsibility had resulted in marked changes. Again, we can only speculate what are the possible limits, but it is unlikely that they have yet been reached.

[10] R. Cooper, 'The Psychology of Boredom', *Science Journal*, February, 1968.
[11] These researches will be published in a subsequent volume.

Chapter 6

THE SUPERVISORS

An essential aim in the whole programme was to achieve the fullest possible involvement of all levels in the plant in the planning and implementing of the scheme. And in this, the supervisors played a key role, as mediators between management and operatives. It was their task to put the principles of the agreement to the men on the shop floor, and in turn to report back on any productivity proposals and suggestions received. But more than this, their own jobs were to be affected in two main ways. Firstly, the proposed shift of responsibility to the operatives would be likely to reduce the number of supervisory staff. More important, the strategy of increasing workers' involvement and participation would call for a radical change in supervisory styles. Furthermore, the agreement involved changes in both the structure of supervision and the numbers of supervisors. Whereas previously there were two grades of Foremen and Assistant Foremen, after the agreement these were replaced by a single tier of supervisors. Finally, the changes resulted in a reduction of about 30 per cent in the numbers of supervisory staff. In short, the implementation of the proposed changes would be likely to generate considerable strains for the first-line supervisors, and make more difficult an already stressful job. How, then, did they react? Were all able to adopt the participatory style? And how close were their perceptions of events to those of the operatives?

Involvement discussion groups
It was the job of the supervisors to help to crystallize shop-floor thinking into concrete proposals for change. What, then, were their own attitudes towards the scheme? At the outset, feelings were mixed. Of the eighteen questioned, only five were optimistic about the outcome and seven were pessimistic. But as the discussions proceeded, more were won over, so that by the

time the scheme was due to be implemented, all but three were in favour.

'I was sceptical at first. I never really thought that operators could be trusted to do all they're doing, in fact. Possibly this was because I've had a Service background and I've always been used to telling/ordering people to do things. I'm glad to say I've been proved wrong.'

'I was suspicious about giving operatives so much responsibility. I was sceptical about the ability of some of them to accept this, simply because we'd become accustomed to checking on them all the time and not trusting them.'

'We tried to involve everybody, to get everybody's ideas and suggestions—this was the thing.'

A major objective of the scheme was to encourage operatives to accept greater responsibility for their work and thus to decrease the amount of close supervision.

'Right from the start the job responsibility and the satisfaction of being your own boss within a team was pushed.'

'This was the great thing because, before the agreement, operatives were checked on by all and sundry, and many of the more intelligent and articulate "ops" rather resented it— they felt they could be trusted. They'd been responsible people in other jobs prior to coming here to do what is a basically tedious and boring job, to be checked on.'

The role of the supervisor

The impact of the changes on the day-to-day work of the supervisors was considerable. For example, before the agreement, assistant foremen were mainly occupied in checking machinery, organizing the allocation of labour and checking operatives' work.

'It was mainly checking operatives on the ways and means of doing the job. They revolved around a ritual—one, two, three steps—if you like, a service routine where you will work to a method. I think the factory at that time was run on a military plan, and we more or less enforced this. They were clockwork doffers. They were given a sheet of paper and it said "at a certain time you will go to a machine and you will doff it in accordance with the methods laid down".'

The post-change situation reveals certain similarities in that checking of operators' work is still carried out by the supervisors, and they are still concerned with team strengths. But there appears to have been a general shift in emphasis from an authority-based role in which rules were enforced and directives given, to a more participative approach characterized by joint discussion and a more personal interest in dealing with the men. Sixteen of the supervisors named this as one of the new components of their role, while two-thirds considered their chief tasks now to be getting to know their team members individually, to guide and advise them about the job, in order to elicit favourable attitudes towards work and the work situation. This 'new mood' is best illustrated by quotations from the supervisors themselves:

'They look to you for guidance, they like somebody there to answer questions. . . . Now they take a lot of decisions themselves, and we have to be prepared to be there for a decision that they've made that they're not quite sure about.'

'Arranging with operatives how we will be loading on the extrusion floor, or whatever it may be, I tell them to plan it out. I discuss things and I agree things with them more frequently now.'

'We have more time for chatting to individuals, either in a group or individually. We're told that man-management is the main thing to think of at the moment. But you've still got a fair amount of technical information to pass through. And there's training and quality checking.'

'There's no question now of any one person in the group having the whip hand—you're all working as one group together. You've got a supervisor who is much more a co-ordinator than an orderer—as he used to be. He used to be a little Fuehrer dashing around giving orders. Not any more;

he's just there to guide things along, to make sure they're going as they should. We look after their welfare of course—that's another important thing. You've got much more time now to devote to anybody's particular problems, and it's surprising how it can help a bloke. You can make him feel you're taking a personal interest, and you'd be surprised how it comes back to you when you want something special done.'

'As supervisors we've got to be very very careful that we don't direct—we must suggest now and let them decide for themselves. . . . Man management is 90 per cent of our job now, and being able to get the correct response.'

However, not all were able to accept the new role without reservations. One at least saw the authority of the foremen as essential, even though it was kept in the background.

'You've still got to be there—the iron fist has got to be shown occasionally to keep things on an even keel . . . it's not because they want to go out there and do work that they do it—it's because I'm there making them do it! There's got to be a driving force there and it's not financial—it's the supervisor behind him.'

What do supervisors feel about these changes in their roles? It appears, on the face of it, that they have lost a number of tasks and responsibilities, leaving a diminished job content and adding a somewhat vague human relations component. However, all but two (both previous foremen) are in favour of the changes. The chief reason—mentioned by eleven of them—is that they are now in close contact with the men, and five former assistant foremen mention increased responsibility as the main source of their approval, as they are now able to make certain decisions which previously would have been made by the foreman.

'More responsibility for men and machines. You've got the authority to take whatever action you want to, whereas before the foreman had it—you didn't.'

But those supervisors who used to be established foremen before the changes do not look at the changes in their roles in the same light. Although, by a process of self-selection, we would have expected the very discontented ones to have left by this time (eleven months after the agreement's implementation), two out of the four interviewed did not declare themselves in favour of the changes; they had mixed feelings about them. They had previously had more status in that they had several assistants and far more operatives under their jurisdiction. And it appears that they experienced far more difficulty in adjusting to their new role. This is borne out by the fact that a number of them left, and the comments of this spinning supervisor are interesting in this context.

'It was an entirely new type of supervision. It was much more difficult for foremen to change. . . . If you was to look at the figures now with people that were established foremen before, how many of them are still left? How many have had nervous breakdowns? This is purely because they just couldn't adapt themselves. This is where a lot of the communications problems arose in the first few months. They didn't want to or they didn't trust their operatives to do things, so information was hogged by them.'

The frank comments of this former established foreman testify to the strain encountered in the process of adaptation:

'I've got a reputation for being fairly hard and fairly brusque, and I'm having to soften down otherwise I'm defeating any object of having a discussion at all. Because my approach in one area wasn't correct I fell down on the job and that's why I was moved into another section. I let the job get a bit on top of me, and I got to the stage where I had to think twice about making the simplest decision which I wouldn't have even thought twice about before. This was my thinking: my authority had been undermined. I ran six assistant foremen and eighty-odd men, and then I was down to a group of thirteen or fourteen men. And my ideas were obviously way out from what they were accustomed to with assistant foremen, and I'm afraid I just didn't get my ideas across, and all I did was build up resentment. I had forgotten how to get the best out of the labour because I hadn't had direct contact with them for so long. I had to change, and change bloody quick or I'd have been gone. . . . My colleague packed up the job altogether—he was an ex-sergeant-major. He lost a packet of weight—the job just got right on top of him. . . . This was the big change; you used to get obedience in the past—maybe a bit grudgingly—but you got it.

'I think some of the satisfaction has gone out of the job simply because a foreman doesn't feel he's as big a man as he was before. But I don't take less satisfaction out of the job now, in fact in many respects I get more—mainly on the man-management side because it gives you a sense of achievement to get over a point of view to sixteen men and get them really believing in what you say.'

However, there is one aspect of the situation which was and still is a source of anxiety. This is the question of future trends in supervision, and their own security.

Supervisors are executives of the policy of their organization. They are less likely to belong to a trade union and have no say in the formulation of policy, so no matter how unpalatable their duties the only alternative to performing them is to leave the organization. Although it seems that there was considerable approval among their ranks for the changes, there had also been general anxiety about their position in the hierarchy when the agreement eventually came in. There was going to be a reorganization which would mean that only a percentage of them could expect to attain the status of established process supervisor. Moreover, in grooming operatives to assume a good many of their duties, it must have occurred to them that they were, up to a point, cutting the ground from under their own feet.

'There still is some anxiety, and I think it's been there ever since the agreement was first mentioned. The operatives regard it as a joke if the supervisor's going to lose his job—they're protected by the union, we're not. When we're talking about the agreement it's: "Oh we'll do your job there's no need for you".'

'The operatives will assume more responsibility in the future, and I think this will lead to a reduction in supervision. We're working ourselves out of a job. This is what it amounts to really. Looking at it impartially, this would be a good thing.'

'If the agreement goes as it should go, the better job one does the nearer one is probably getting to cutting one's own throat. But it's so far in the future that it doesn't do any good to worry about it.'

'I can see that in the next couple of years supervision will be practically a thing of the past in the sense that we've known it. Let's face it, one man is doing what half a dozen were doing twelve months ago.'

Foremen and assistants: relationships and communications

While relationship between foremen and assistant foremen were, in the main, satisfactory before the agreement, there were sources of discontent. Former assistants complained about lack of information coming from the foreman, disagreement with him about the selection of 'probation' supervisors, his unwillingness to delegate decisions, favouritism, and so on.

'The foreman would expect you, as an assistant, to go out and chase up all these things that were going wrong. This is where discussions would have been a great help. Instead of saying, "look, we've got a problem here, what are we going to do about it?" they'd say, "this is bloody wrong, get out and do something about it . . .". You had some foremen who were still the type of people with bowler hats and walking sticks—you know, "I know it all, you know nothing".

'Friction arose simply because we were in this awkward position where we couldn't make decisions. We had to run to them for the answers to silly questions, and quite often you would get an answer which they knew very well was wrong, and it was frustrating. Precisely the same thing as you had between operatives and assistant foremen because there wasn't this trust. It was just lack of communications between people.'

The foreman was the last link in the chain of communication between management and assistant foreman, and although only two respondents considered that communications between them and their foreman were poor, most former assistant foremen pointed to inadequacies in this system. And there is some evidence that in the past, foremen withheld information as a strategy for strengthening their position.

'The thermex system is a bit complex—putting it on and off a pair of machines. Well, this sort of job was always done by the foreman and it was like a little guarded secret!'

'In some respects the communications before the agreement was appalling. As regards like the technical side of things where technical information was being passed to the foreman which never even reached the assistant foreman, so it never got out on the floor at all.'

'Just prior to the agreement the foreman was getting a lot of information from the assistant works manager down, and a lot of it wasn't being passed on to the assistant foreman. I think they were a little bit more doubtful about the agreement than we were. We knew there was a chance of promotion whereas the foremen knew it wouldn't mean promotion for them. So whether they were thinking, "Well, we've got to go out on the shop floor and the more I know about it the better". I couldn't say.'

'Some of them fancied a bit of one-upmanship, and they kept the information to themselves. It was all so childish— what good did it do them? The system wasn't brilliant but it was links in the system that spoilt the system. It was so stupid and it caused no end of trouble. . . . Bits of technical information—"we know a little bit more than you" sort of thing. . . . A lot of people in the old days said we were like mushrooms—kept in the dark and fed on you-know-what!'

Discussion and conclusion

The adoption of a supervisory style based on participation was not easy. For all supervisors, it meant a threat to their status and security; for some, the fundamental changes in behaviour required were more than they could manage. Some had left, and others had experienced severe strain in adjusting to the demands of the new style, with its shift in emphasis from authority and directives to participatory leadership.

However, the general impression is that the majority had not only accepted but preferred the new role—at least, of those of the original supervisors who remained. This is very important for the success of any changes of this kind. For their success, such styles depend on the genuine commitment of supervisors. The danger is that a switch to a human relations style may be perceived as manipulation and generate evasion and hostility.[1] But in any case, there are limits to the results of a switch to an employee-centred approach. As previous chapters have shown, the technology militated against job interest and involvement. Nevertheless, within these limits the impact of supervisory changes was significant.

[1] C. Argyris, *Integrating the Individual and the Organization* (1964), pp. 110–12.

Chapter 7

ATTITUDES TO CHANGE

It will be remembered that the agreement was seen as more than simply a productivity bargain. It was hoped that the preliminary discussions would bring about a significant modification in attitudes towards the job—away from the preoccupation with nicely calculated rewards for discrete quanta of effort and towards a greater willingness to accept responsibility for the overall execution of the job following the abolition of detailed and close supervision. In short, the reorganization offered the promise of job enlargement and job enrichment and of a greater intrinsic interest in the job.

The considerable success in achieving such objectives has been documented in earlier chapters. Management had attached a good deal of importance to the preliminary involvement discussions. These had included attempts to familiarize operatives and supervisors with those recent theories in the social and behavioural sciences which had influenced management thinking.[1] What then was the effect of such discussions? Or was this like any other wage-effort bargain, one which was entered into mainly for the promise of higher pay?

Involvement discussions

Involvement discussions were the chief medium for communicating information about the productivity agreement and canvassing the ideas and opinions of workers about the changes: 70 per cent of operatives named them as their chief source of

---

[1] In fact, supervisors were exposed to social science theories to a far greater extent than were operatives. In order to measure the impact on operatives of exposure to these ideas each was asked whether at any time he could remember anybody talking about what makes a worker happy or satisfied at work, or discussing the rewards of more interesting and responsible work. All but one, who in fact had been in a more technical job and not an operator at the time, replied in the negative. This line of questioning was, of course, necessary because if the theories had had a big influence then this would indicate the possibility of a 'Hawthorne effect' contaminating our results.

information. Essentially, the rationale of involvement is that those who are going to be most affected by changes should participate in deciding what those changes should be. The main advantage of this for attitudes to innovation, so the argument goes, is that participants will feel that they are being consulted and involved in making decisions which will affect them—that they are parties to the change and not merely recipients of it. It is hoped that this will avoid feelings of being manipulated, of powerlessness to influence a course of events which may change one's work role and situation quite radically. Suggestions must be judged on their merits and rational explanations offered if for any reason they are found to be unworkable or inexpedient. This is important if commitment to the changes is not to be jeopardized in what is unavoidably a political situation.[2] But how effective was this strategy in inducing favourable responses to the agreement? Operatives were asked how much influence they considered they had had in deciding the changes.

Table 7.1: *Amount of influence in deciding changes*

	%
Large amount	28·3
Fair amount	33·4
Little or none	23·3
Don't know	15·0
	100·0 $(N = 60)$

Just over 60 per cent considered that they had had at least a fair amount of influence (Table 7.1) and their remarks indicate more fully the significance of their replies. The first quotation is from an operative who attended as many as twenty involvement discussions:

> 'Supervision listened to proposals from the shop floor and if they didn't agree they gave good reasons. In my estimation it was thrashed out quite fair.'

> 'The management decided the changes and it was up to the workers to say yes or no.'

[2] A number of previous researches support the view that effective change requires full participation in the decision-making process. See, for example, J. R. P. French in L. Kahn and E. Boulding, *Power and Conflict in Organizations* (1964).

'The chargehand gave us all the gen and if we didn't agree with the things he told us might happen we told the way we thought would be best.'

But the following comment gives the other side of the coin:

'It was all worked out before-hand. They just checked our suggestions against a list they had already prepared.'

Table 7.2: *Attendance at involvement discussions is related to perceptions of their influence*

Influence	No. of discussions attended		
	0–2	3–4	5+
	%	%	%
Much or fair	57	77	88
Little or none	43	23	12
	100	100	100
	(21)	(13)	(17)

The greater the number of meetings attended, the more the influence they believed they had (Table 7.2). However, we must interpret this association with caution. It is possible that the more highly involved and co-operative workers would attend meetings more frequently.

In this whole process of change, as we have seen, the supervisors played a key role in running the involvement discussions and in mediating the plans of high management. In the experience of some of the supervisors, the discussions undoubtedly contributed to a change of attitude:

'Initially on my shift they weren't prepared to discuss the manpower changes without the payment structure. It took about three weeks and then the thing swung the other way—they were all diving to get in on it. Some of the things they were prepared to do I doubt if I would have tackled. The swing over was really amazing. It was fantastic the constructive suggestions, the constructive criticism about the way the place was running at the moment.'

'They took a long time to come on; people were still apprehensive in the early stages of saying too much. They were frightened they were going to tell somebody something they didn't want to go to a wrong place; they were frightened their own mates would sit on them for saying something. In this place there's a seven-and-a-half year barrier to break down; there's always been an "us" and "them". And with this completely new concept it wanted a lot of really driving home. But I think now it's paying dividends. People are realizing they can talk and that by talking to you they can get a lot more done. The atmosphere is a lot freer. Whereas you went into a room originally and said your piece and threw it open to the floor—a great stoney silence. Now people are jumping in before you've even finished.'

Operatives not only became involved in proposals for change, but felt that they had played a part in shaping them. Consequently, there was greater willingness to accept the changes when they came:

'I think the meetings were invaluable, and we were holding them right up to the time we came in one morning and they said, "Right, you're on the agreement". It was in the wind but it came in just like that. It was fantastic really to see the way everybody knuckled down and it all fitted in.'

'I would say the agreement wouldn't have gone so smoothly without discussions. Once they'd agreed to something it was in, no question about it, whereas before you had a little slip of paper saying "this is going to happen with effect from Monday". You could do the same thing now and you'd get that rebellious reaction immediately. If someone puts a little extra work on you or alters the system without involving you in it you'll say, "What the hell do they want to alter that for?" But if you go to a group and *ask* them, they come up with what you've got written down anyway, and they say, "Right then, we'll start that on Monday". And this is the secret I think.'

But the discussions appear to have been successful in another direction. A number of supervisors and operatives remarked on the ease with which most workers slipped into their new roles. Several supervisors believed that the transition went so smoothly because of the prior preparation at involvement discussions. The comment of the supervisor already quoted is typical: 'It was fantastic really to see the way everybody knuckled down and it all fitted in.'

There is little doubt then· that the involvement discussions paved the way and facilitated the smooth introduction of the agreement. But this does not mean that the operatives had necessarily accepted management's definition of the changes, and in particular, the promise of a more interesting and responsible job. What, in fact, did the operatives expect to get out of the agreement? Were they attracted primarily by the promise of higher pay? Or did the possibility of a more interesting job have any pull?

The Attractions of the Agreement

The over-riding conclusion we came to was the predominantly instrumental orientation to work. Like the Luton workers,[3] these men were attracted to their job primarily by the relatively high rates of pay, and saw high pay as some compensation for the boredom, noise, and inconvenience of shift work. Most (61·7 per cent) were satisfied with the pay. But while increased pay was mentioned most frequently as the main attraction of the agreement (Table 7.3), a sizeable proportion (25 per cent) associated expected improvements in pay with the anticipation of greater interest and responsibility. Some were willing to accept the agreement solely on the basis of higher pay, but came to appreciate the other benefits later on, while others who originally saw nothing to attract them, were won over when the changes came into operation. In short, it looks as though the involvement discussions had had *some* impact, but for the majority, the *initial* attraction of the agreement was the pay.

Table 7.3: *Expected benefits from the agremeent*

	%
Pay	41·7
Job interest and responsibility + pay	25·0
Nothing	33·3
	100·0 ($N = 60$)

[3] J. Goldthorpe, *et. al.*, *The Affluent Worker: Industrial Attitudes and Behaviour* (1968).

'The thing was the money, but as soon as we got to know more about it, it started to throw new light on the job altogether.'

'I think the main thing was getting a little bit of authority and using your own initiative. And, of course, a bit of extra money.'

'Money was the first thing that appealed—and that you could be trusted to do the job.'

'I was getting a bit bored and I thought it would be more interesting and help the time to pass quicker.'

An interesting feature of the replies from workers who found no aspects of the agreement attractive is that many of them were agreeably surprised by the changes.

'They used to say you are going to get more responsibility and I always re-phrased this as "more work". As it turns out, the responsibility is there. But everybody was wary about it before it came in.'

Attitudes Towards Change

Not all were equally favourable to the changes. Two factors were considered which might explain the greater willingness of some to accept the agreement. Firstly, those who had previously experienced changes which had been rewarding, or at least acceptable. We tested this by exploring operatives' perceptions of the frequency of past technical and organizational change. Forty-five per cent replied that change had taken place rarely or not at all during their years with the company, whereas 55 per cent replied that changes had been brought in fairly often or often. Of those who had had enough experience of change for useful comment (i.e. 65 per cent of the entire sample), 53 per cent favoured past changes. The remaining 12 per cent consisted mainly of operatives who were indifferent. This fairly high percentage of operatives who had had favourable experience of change would appear to create a situation favourable to further innovation. In the following comments we shall see the kind of change that had taken place prior to the productivity agreement, and the reasons for the workers' attitudes towards it:

'The production of nylon when I started eight years ago was crude compared to what it is today. It's an industry where there is continuous change . . . it's more efficient. It means that yarn is produced more cheaply, which means putting the firm on a more stable basis—which makes our jobs more secure.'

'The process changes day by day—a job you're doing today is out tomorrow and something else is in . . . it's progress; you've got to expect it and accept it.

'One thing was progressive to stationary doffing. When I first started here the 134 process had a running time of 5 hours 20 minutes. And you've got twin biscuits in spinning which cut the time by half—so you've got four times the amount of work in the same time. . . . There have been improvements as regarding everything. You get more money—you do more work for it, but that's fair enough.'

'If you don't have change you probably won't have a job. In this industry it's pretty tight; if they don't keep up with the the next firm they go down.'

Several comments such as these, displayed an awareness of the reality of competition, equating job security with the competitive position of the enterprise. It is perhaps surprising at first that security is mentioned as a reason for favouring changes, since the worker's attitude to technical change and rationalization is commonly held to be one of fear of redundancy—with consequent resistance. At any rate, whether or not this was an important factor in shaping attitudes to the agreement, it is evident that management at least had no great wall of resistance to surmount such as might be expected in more traditionally militant industries.

Another possible factor influencing willingness to accept the changes is age. We found a strong relationship between age and intention to stay in present job[4] (Table 7.4). The reasons for

[4] There were differences in the age distribution for different sections. Analysis within sections of attachment related to age indicates that age is an important variable accounting for differences in attachment.

this are, on the whole, fairly obvious. As far as a career is concerned, our young workers seem to be somewhat confused, not liking particularly the job they are in but not having their sights set on any other occupation. The pay attracted them to this job and it is enough to hold them for a while, but they do not regard it as being a long-term prospect. There is too little interest for most of them, and since pay is related to length of service (or the time it takes them to become fully trained and competent) and not to age, they are at the top of the wage scale and there is virtually no chance of further individual financial advancement.

By contrast, most older workers, i.e. those within about fifteen years of retirement, are satisfied with a relatively secure and well-paid job which provides a pension. They simply feel that nowhere else would they obtain such favourable conditions, even supposing they could get a job at all at their time of life. And so they are, generally speaking, reasonably contented to spend the remaining years of their working life in their present job.

Workers in the intermediate years divide into almost equal groups, 53 per cent of them intending to stay and 47 per cent intending to leave or being unsure. In common with the 21–30 years group, an opportunistic orientation to work was frequently encountered among those who do not definitely intend to stay; a readiness to leave if a 'better' (not necessarily better paid) job turned up.

'I would leave if I could get a job with anything like the money.' (Age 22.)

'There is no future here for me. I'd like to be in the position to take a drop in earnings when I would do something mundane, like a policeman or ambulance driver, bringing you into contact with people more.' (Age 24.)

'If the right opportunity comes along with the same money, I'd probably take it.' (Age 30.)

'If I could get another job with more money I'd go tomorrow. I'm in this world to better myself.' (Age 33.)

'They'll have to sack me to get rid of me!' (Age 42.)

'I've got fifteen years working life ahead of me, and when that's up I'm paying to a pension scheme and I've got some security.' (Age 50.)

Table 7.4 : *Age in relation to future job plans*

Age	% intends staying	% intends leaving or D/K
21–30	8	92 = 100%
31–40	40	60
41–50	73	27
51+	81	19
	($p = 0 \cdot 01$) ($N = 60$)	

Finally, what were attitudes towards further change? A substantial proportion (42 per cent) were in favour (Table 7.5).

Table 7.5 : *Attitudes towards further change*

	%
In favour	41·7
Against or indifferent	36·6
Not possible or don't know	21·7
	100·0 ($N = 60$)

Those in favour of further change gave a variety of reasons, referring mainly to extrinsic attractions (money and security) although some gave interest and responsibility:

'Any change always means more money.'

'I think the more jobs you've got to do, the more interest there is in the job.'

'The more work they give you to do, the less slack time you've got, and the time goes quicker.'

'If you've got more responsibility you take more interest in the job.'

'I think in three months' time I shall be so bored with it that any change will be acceptable.'

'These improvements have got to come—they can't stand still or the firm wouldn't be in business long. If changes did come along we'd have to fall in with them, and if it was better for us we'd all go along with it.'

Although during the interviews no great wave of excitement at the mention of further changes was encountered, no very strong resistance was met with either. It would appear that the impact of the changes has not been so great as to arouse very pronounced general responses one way or the other. However, we have noted differences between areas in attitudes to several factors, and a correlation of attitudes to further change with area worked in yields an interesting result (Table 7.6):

Table 7.6 : *Attitudes to further change differ between sections*

	In favour %	Against or indifferent %	
Spinning	80	20	$(N = 15)$
Drawtwist	37	63	$(N = 19)$
Auxiliary	46	54	$(N = 13)$
			$(p = 0\cdot05)$

It can be seen that further change is viewed far more favourably by workers in the spinning section than by auxiliary and drawtwist operatives, the latter being the least in favour. As we have indicated earlier, and will examine more fully in the final chapter, the general level of dissatisfaction is highest in the drawtwist area, springing largely from its unfavourable physical surroundings. It is not surprising that the group who are most dissatisfied, and who have gained least from the agreement, are least in favour of further changes of the kind which have done little to remove their main source of complaint—the noise of the drawtwist area.

These findings are in line with other researches. Chinoy,[5] for instance, postulates a chronology of aspirations. Young workers seek immediate gratifications. They are not interested in advancement, and their conception of the future is a very short-term one. They see the automobile factory as providing a temporary means to extrinsic rewards, but have nebulous thoughts about something better presenting itself in an indeter-

[5] E. Chinoy, *Automobile Workers and the American Dream* (1955), particularly Chapter 9.

minate future. Although marriage may stimulate ambition, their lack of skill and qualifications, and family financial obligations limit their chances of advancement outside the factory. By middle age and beyond, any aspirations they once had are modified as they settle down to the reality of their situation. Small goals within the factory and the security that comes with length of service take the place of earlier dreams of small business ownership and the like.

Chapter 8

THE IMPACT ON PRODUCTIVITY
AND MORALE

So far, we have discussed mainly the impact of the agreement on work attitudes and satisfactions. But the object of the exercise was also to achieve the more effective utilization of manpower through a more flexible use of operatives and supervisors. What then was the pay-off? What was the saving on actual manning of machines? And was there any effect on the quality as well as quantity of output?

The Effect on the Labour Force

During 1966/7 output was declining so that by the end of 1967, the plant was running at only 75–80 per cent of capacity. During this same period, the process labour force was allowed to run down by natural wastage so that it had declined by 23 per cent by December 1967 from 1997 to 1517. Immediately after the introduction of the agreement in January 1968, the plant returned to full capacity. The output increased by 20 per cent compared with the end of 1966, but with a labour force some 20 per cent smaller. Moreover, during 1968 a new section was started. But there was no external recruitment until the middle of 1969.

Some assessment can be made of the contribution of the various changes resulting from the agreement:

1. Elimination of non-essential work, and revised methods (i.e. different, more flexible work methods)
   $= 15 \cdot 1$ per cent

2. Re-allocation of work. For example, in one auxiliary section, reorganization and consolidation of the work has reduced the need to transport materials $= 5 \cdot 1$ per cent

3. Changes in work measurement standards. The original measurements over-estimated labour requirements
$$= 3 \cdot 8 \text{ per cent}$$

4. The number of maintenance workers has been reduced by between 14 and 15 per cent, in spite of extra machinery which would otheriwise have required an increase of twelve men. The savings in process and maintenance supervision are around 30 per cent.

Labour Turnover

But the reduction in overall numbers is not the only saving. There is also evidence of a more stable work-force with a decline in labour turnover. During the period January to December 1967, the monthly average turnover was $1 \cdot 36$ per cent. During 1968, the first year of the agreement, the figure was $0 \cdot 43$ per cent. A third of our respondents reported that they felt more like staying because of the productivity deal. Although the increase in pay emerges as a paramount importance, changes in job content and increased satisfaction have also helped.

The more stable workforce is obviously desirable in an organization in which the workers have a number of skills which facilitate their transferability from one job to another. The point was often made that a new recruit to the factory would require far more training now than he would have done before the changes were implemented. Moreover, as we have already noted, there was a more favourable attitude towards technical change and job mobility within the factory than one would expect to find in many other industries. This is of utmost importance in this particular industry which is highly competitive and relies on continuing technical improvement and an increasingly efficient use of labour resources to maintain or improve its competitive position.

Absenteeism

On the other hand, absenteeism has increased. Comparing 1967 with 1968, the hours lost as a percentage of the planned working time were $5 \cdot 7$ and $6 \cdot 19$ respectively. This slight increase is mainly explainable by the improved sickness benefits which are now more or less on a par with those paid to staff. For example, full-pay is given for periods of absence ranging between four and twenty-six weeks per year depending on length of service, and a certain number of days of uncertified sickness leave is now allowed. Indeed, a man may be several pounds a week better off when sick than when at work. In view of these more favourable conditions it could be argued that an increase of 0·47 per cent, although obviously undesirable, is less than might have been anticipated. But whether this figure would have been higher had these extra benefits been conferred without the changes in organization and the consequent changes in job satisfaction is a matter of speculation.

Operative Performance

Both conversion efficiency (the amount of first-grade yarn produced from a given quantity of polymer) and machine efficiency have improved with the changes. Again, it is not easy to say which variables contributed to this effect. In addition to the possible effects of changes in satisfaction on operatives' performance, technical improvements have unquestionably increased efficiency. To take an example from the extrusion floor, polymer is necessarily wasted when the packs through which it is extruded are changed. But these packs have been improved to give them a longer life, and consequently the frequency with which they are changed is reduced. This reduces polymer wastage and hence gives greater conversion efficiency. Similarly, with regard to machine efficiency, the introduction of bigger 'cake' sizes has reduced the doffing frequency and hence the time during which the machine is not running. The switch from scheduled doffing to a free-queuing system has also considerably reduced 'down-time' or the periods during which the machines are standing idle.

Thus, increased conversion and machine efficiency cannot be directly attributable to changes in attitudes to the job. However, it is problematic whether certain of these technical changes would have been accepted by the operatives outside this general context of change. Certainly, resistance was encountered in the past to increasing 'cake' sizes. The informed view of a member of senior management is that, although a falling off in conversion efficiency through a relaxing of work standards, less stringent checking etc., was the price they expected to pay, they were agreeably surprised that no significant decline had taken place as a result of a deterioration in operatives' performance. Incidentally, it is technical changes such as these which contribute to labour savings: less frequent pack-changing and doffing will obviously reduce the work load for a shrinking labour force.

Such objective evidence is supported by the more subjective assessments of the impact of the agreement on output, based mainly on the judgement of the supervisors. There was general agreement that more work was, in fact, being done, due mainly to the increase in flexibility in working arrangements.

> 'They're doing more production work and a lot of the silly little jobs and frustrating jobs have been take off them. You know, if before you had a team doing nothing for an hour, it was just a question of finding them something to do—we used to get them sweeping up the floor, picking things up off the floor. This wasn't producing anything.'

But if more was being turned out, there is also some impressionistic evidence that there was more real free time than before. As we discussed in Chapter 2, there are many examples in the literature of the strategies adopted by workers to increase their own control over the pace and amount of work. By making an extra effort, for example, output can be piled up to allow a slackening of effort or a period of rest. Such strategies reduce the monotony; the promise of a rest is a motivation to effort. It is not surprising to find evidence of such 'gold-bricking' among our sample of operatives engaged in predominantly boring and monotonous work. And it is quite possible for such a redistribution of work effort—intensive work followed by rest—to be consistent with maintaining a high overall level of output. The strategy serves mainly to make a boring job tolerable. Moreover, such rest time, freely chosen, is qualitatively different from prescribed and fixed periods. Indeed, one factor which may have contributed to the decline in the boredom of the job may have been precisely this increased freedom for 'gold-bricking'. The very perceptive remarks of one supervisor support this interpretation:

'I think they're doing a bit more work simply because the system is that much better and allows them to do more work. They couldn't do more work in very many cases before; they couldn't deviate from the schedule. . . . There is a certain incentive in working a bit harder, and I don't think money's got anything to do with it. . . . There's only one real incentive in drawtwist at the moment and that is time. They can, by their own efforts, by working that much harder, alter their frequency of work which allows them a period between the machine stopping. They can do two machines in half an hour and they've got half an hour to themselves. They go well over their fifty-seven minutes' break[1] simply because they can so regulate their work that there isn't any more work to do. . . . They feel they've made something—they create this time when *they* want it. Under the old set-up they had to take this time because they couldn't do nothing about it. They create these gaps by working harder or slower to have their rest periods or meal breaks.'

Operatives, too, felt that they were now doing more work. None felt that they had been doing too much before the agreement. Indeed, 35 per cent thought they were then doing too little. Now, 88·3 per cent considered they were doing more work, 10 per cent the same amount and 1·7 per cent thought that less was being done. Moreover, few felt that the extra work was obligatory (Table 8.1).

Table 8.1: *Whether extra work felt to be obligatory*

	%
Voluntary	33·3
Involuntary	11·7
Both	31·7
Don't know	23·3
	100 ($N = 60$)

Greater interest and responsibility were among the explanations offered for this increased effort.

[1] The break for meals was 30 minutes. But an additional 27 minutes in rest periods could be taken during the shift.

'We do more work now; all the jobs are varied jobs and it makes more interest.'

'We understand now that we've got more responsibility and we accept this, and know if we make an error we're going to get told off—which is fair enough since we're getting more money. We do more work because we're pretty conscientious, and being able to do the job your way instead of being told "do that with your left hand and that with your right".'

'I think if people are left alone they carry on a lot better. If anybody didn't want to do much they could definitely get away with it.'

'People want more money—that's what's behind it.'

However, the most frequent reason given brings us back to a very familiar theme:

'You don't have to (work harder) but it passes the time a lot quicker.'

'Before, you did your machine and you had five or ten minutes over so you went and had a smoke. I found I was spending more time having a smoke than what I was working on the machine. Whereas now, you start a machine and you go on to the next one, or have five or ten minutes off when you want it—providing you have only fifty-six minutes in the shift. You're obviously doing more now because you haven't got a card to go by—you've just got the big graph. Obviously some blokes are getting out of it and not doing so much as they should do, but others are. If you can work and stick at it, home is going to come that much nearer, isn't it? I found yesterday that I was going so fast that I lost track of time.'

'We're not working much harder, it's just that instead of waiting for a machine's starting-up time we go straight on to another machine.'

'We had a quantity to do and once that was done there were days when you had time over—perhaps half an hour—when you could have done more. . . . There are a few who would take advantage but not the majority who carry on and

I

do the job as it should be done. They're getting a fair wage now, and I think the majority think "I'll do a fair day's work for that wage". I know for a fact that every man there is turning out a lot more boxes than he did under the incentive scheme; half as many again in some cases. I find that the day goes much quicker.'

Quality and the incentive scheme

It will be remembered that with the pre-agreement incentive scheme, a bonus was awarded and then deductions were made for mistakes or poor quality output. With the introduction of the agreement, both the 'negative-incentive', and the quality patrollers who enforced it were abolished.

As we have seen, the great majority (75 per cent) thought that the incentive scheme had been ineffective in achieving its objective of maintaining quality. But it must be stressed that considerable efforts had in any case been exerted to make operatives quality conscious. In short, it would seem that it was an awareness of the importance of quality rather than the incentive scheme as such which was important.

> 'It's been built into us that it's the quality that sells the yarn, and if we're not doing the job properly we're not getting the quality. We're not more careless now than we were before.'

So, for spinners and drawtwisters the removal of the scheme has resulted in a drop in dissatisfaction with what many thought to be an unfair imposition, but no one reported a deterioration in quality. The results for auxiliary workers present a more interesting picture. Several operatives spoke about the cheating to which it was open, and said that there was more carelessness over quality then than now:

> 'I think incentives induced more carelessness in some respects. They used to be out for the bonus and not bother about the quality. A lot of people I know for a fact were careless and didn't do the job properly.'

> 'It encouraged fiddling. If somebody had a quantity to do he might do the job inefficiently to fulfil his quota. The agree-

ment has stopped that. Now that we work as a team, shirkers are given a kick by their team-mates.'

Morale

Finally, we turn to more general impressions on overall feelings about the changes. Operatives were asked whether, taking everything into consideration, they felt any happier about their job as a result of the agreement.

Table 8.2 : *Impact of agreement on overall happiness with job*

	%
Much happier	6·7
Happier	56·6
A little happier	11·7
No different	25·0
	100·0

First, we will illustrate the remarks of the twenty-two in the last two categories who are little or no happier:

> 'I like the money more, but that's only on paper. I get about ten bob a week clear after tax. I'm not really interested in the job at all. I suppose 90 per cent of the time I'm here I'm thinking about something else. Today, I've been wondering whether I've got a valve gone in the car and whether I can find out without having to take the head off.'

> 'I think most men come to work for money. It's not very interesting. I find it a bit more interesting. We've had these changes before but once you got used to them you were back to square one again.'

Those in the first two groups who feel happier mentioned money, interest, job enlargement, responsibility and team-work.

> 'I think there's a much better feeling on the plant now between men and between men and supervision. I think everybody thinks they've got a part to play and they're prepared to play it.'

> 'The time goes quicker, we're getting more money and we're doing more work.'

'It's come home to you more what the job's all about, I think. Before we were doing a job—doffing—and that was the end of that. But now you've got more to think about, to do. All the minor jobs are wrapped into one. . . . Machine checking is one thing that brings the job home to you quite a lot because you're looking for things when you're doffing now that you didn't do before. I suppose I'm happier now because you know you can go up a grade if you're prepared to put effort into it.'

'You feel freer. Nobody's going to interfere with you providing you do a decent day's work. It's totally different now.'

A further index of general satisfaction is the change in attitudes towards leaving. Before the agreement, more than half had considered leaving, 30 per cent seriously. After the agreement, one third felt more like staying.

One final index of the impact of the changes is the impressions of supervisors on the overall morals in the plant. We have already quoted ample evidence on the generally increased levels of satisfaction among operatives, and the greater sense of participation and involvement, leading to closer team-work and improved relations between operatives and supervisors. If these are indices of morale, then certainly, the improvement was marked.

With one exception, all the supervisors we spoke to agreed that there had been a change in the general atmosphere in the plant:

'Most of them are far happier with the job. I know chaps who, before the agreement, would see something wrong and be "blind". Now, he'd either draw my attention to it if it's something he can't deal with, or if he can deal with it, he will.'

'There's been a vast improvement. At times before the agreement there was a black cloud hanging over the plant— this is quite true. You could almost cut it with a knife. It hasn't been there since the agreement. Why, I don't know. People would say things, it would build up into something out of all proportion to what it really was, and you had the devil's own job to really shift it.'

Chapter 9

CONCLUSIONS AND DISCUSSION

How far then were the expectations of management realized?
And how far do our findings confirm the views of the behavioural
and social scientists which influenced the aims and strategies of
the productivity agreement?

Savings in Manning

It must be stressed at the outset that before the exercise
started local management was satisfied that it had reached a
high level of efficiency. Comparisons with other plants showed
that only in the USA was there tighter manning. For some time
sophisticated work study and work measurement techniques
had already been employed. Management was, therefore,
frankly sceptical whether there was much room for improvement. Yet it had been possible to return to full production
(100 per cent of capacity) and to start up a new section with a
labour force 24 per cent lower than it had been in 1966. Indeed
it was not until July 1969 that any further recruitment occurred.

There is no doubt that it was only through the medium of the
productivity deal that such savings were achieved. As we have
seen from the evidence of the survey, once the involvement
discussions got under way, the operatives generally responded
positively and enthusiastically. It was here that the suggestions
were made for savings on manning—suggestions which in some
cases were far more daring than supervisors would have thought
it possible to make. Indeed, it could be argued that it was the
decision to involve the operatives in the process of change
which was of crucial importance. Not that such involvement
had overwhelming support—on either side—to start with.
Certainly, there were many in management who were not only
doubtful about the possibility of further improvements in
manning, but were equally sceptical about the wisdom of

increasing shop-floor involvement—doubtful, that is, that the shop floor could contribute anything useful.

Motivation and Satisfaction

The operatives too, approached the exercise with caution. In spite of management's emphasis on the need for preliminary education in the Herzbergian theory of motivation—that it is the job itself which is the source of positive satisfaction—the initial attraction was increased pay. The operatives would appear to have been overwhelmingly 'hygiene-seekers'.

Yet once the involvement discussions were under way, their latent interest in the job itself emerged. And once the new workings had been introduced, the more intrinsic rewards became apparent to many. There is no doubt that there was a major pay-off in terms of decreased boredom. And most welcomed the increase in responsibility, some seeing it as marking the end of personal stagnation and offering for the first time the chance for self-realization and personal growth in work.

There is not necessarily a contradiction here. None *expected* the job to be interesting when they took it. And similarly, few expected much initially from the agreement except an improved effort bargain. What *is* interesting, and most significant, is the emergence of latent needs for self-actualization. Despite years of work with little responsibility, the majority accepted the opportunity, even welcomed it when offered. Such evidence lends guarded support to the view that those who work in factories are capable of substantial development. Apathy, irresponsibility, laziness and the like are, at least to some extent, the result of past management policies which have functioned as self-fulfilling prophecies. In other words, we cannot deduce from the fact that workers appear to be attracted mainly by the money that their involvement in work is purely instrumental. Our evidence shows that there are latent needs which surface when there are opportunities for their satisfaction.

The gains were real. But they were also limited. The main result was the reduction in boredom rather than any major increase in the intrinsic interest in the job. The most important change was the substitution of free-queuing for the scheduled doffing in the drawtwist area and the corresponding changes in other areas. There was less hanging about and the work did make better use of abilities. There was a greater feeling of being in control.

However, basically the job was unchanged. There had been some significant degree of job-enlargement, but this hardly amounted to any substantial job-enrichment, if we mean by this an increase in the complexity of the work, calling for greater skills: 38 per cent still found the work little or no more interesting. Indeed, of the 62 per cent who reported more interest, it was clear that for many this simply meant less boring. In short, the changes amounted to a marked decrease in dissatisfaction rather than to a positive increase in satisfaction. Certainly, by contrast with operatives in highly automated plant which we were investigating at the same time, there was a marked difference in the over-all level of satisfaction.

There is one point that we would wish to stress. Most of our respondents had never had the opportunity for self-actualizing work. And the modest improvements which they experienced were a source of considerable satisfaction. But there were some, albeit a minority, who had previously been employed in more skilled jobs, and who had deliberately traded intrinsic interest for pay.[1] For these, as we have seen, the improvements were minimal. The importance of previous experience on expectations and satisfactions underlines our earlier point that the lack of any positive motivation owes much to previous socialization.[2]

Herzberg Reconsidered

Two implications for Herzberg's theory are immediately apparent. Firstly, one major focus of dissatisfaction centred on the job-content rather than on hygiene factors. Secondly, the increased effort stemmed to a significant extent from an avoidance need—to escape from boredom—rather than from any positive search for self-actualization. It is to avoid boredom that they do more work. Thirdly, these men were consciously trading the relatively high pay of the job for the disadvantages of shift work, noise and boredom. Indeed, some men had left

---

[1] Similarly, some of the Luton workers had been attracted away from much more intrinsically rewarding jobs. J. Goldthorpe, *et. al.*, *op. cit.* (1968).

[2] On the deadening effect of school experience, see M. Carter, *Home, School and Work* (1962).

more interesting jobs for the higher pay packets of the nylon spinners. In such circumstances, pay assumes particular significance as a course of satisfaction. Whereas Herzberg considers dissatisfaction with pay derived from a sense of unfairness with the wage system in the organization, in our case it usually implied inadequate compensation for contextual factors.

On the other hand, Herzberg's view that contextual factors stand in the way of positive self-actualization has some support. For many, physical conditions were the source of strong, even intense dissatisfaction. But how far preoccupation with avoidance needs bars the way to the satisfaction of motivational needs is difficult to say, though some of the comments we received suggest that this may be a possibility for many.

In short, useful though it is, Herzberg's distinction between motivators and satisfiers does not entirely hold up.[3] Men can work hard to *avoid* dissatisfaction. And they may derive positive satisfaction from high pay where this is consciously sought as compensation for the lack of intrinsic rewards.

Technology and the Limits of Organizational Change

In any socio-technical system, the technology sets the parameters for organizational change. What is remarkable about this experiment is how much could be achieved through relatively small organizational changes. But the limits are there. It is the constraints of the technology which underlies the limits to job enlargement and job-enrichment. Whether the limits have yet been reached remains to be seen. But the pervading influence of the technology emerged particularly dramatically in the marked differences between the three main areas in the plant. Hence, we have workers in the same company, with the same management and the same productivity agreement and broad pattern of organizational changes. Yet it is above all the noise of the drawtwist area which underlies the generally higher dissatisfaction of the drawtwist operatives which we have frequently noticed in this inquiry[4] (Table 9.1). This higher dissatisfaction, it will be remembered, spilled over into

[3] There are a number of studies criticizing Herzberg's 'two-factor' theory. But such criticisms do not mean that the distinction is not a useful one.

[4] Nevertheless, operatives don't, in fact, want to move to, say, spinning.

quite markedly different attitudes towards who benefits from the agreement (Chapter 4).

Table 9.1: *Dissatisfaction by area*

	No. of context factors with which dissatisfied		
	0–3	4–7	8–11
	%	%	% = 100% (60)
Drawtwist	46	46	8
Spinning	50	39	11
Auxiliary	72	17	11

Despite the best efforts of management, the job remained essentially alienating, though considerably less so than before. Workers enjoyed a significant increase in control over their activities, but compared with workers in automated plants, it is the machines which control them rather than they the machines. The job for most is essentially meaningless, though more could be done here by visits and fuller information to put the fractionized tasks in a wider context. But it is at the level of self-actualization that the limitations of technology are most apparent. Despite job-enlargement, the worker remains a hand, investing little skill, and having comparatively little involvement. It is in this sense that he is estranged from the processes and the product; his work is separated from his self. He is alienated.

Labour Relations and the Effort-bargain

A major objective of this agreement was to achieve a significant change in labour relations. Considerable hopes were pinned on the new status of the operatives as salaried staff. It was anticipated that this would go some way towards encouraging the unity or teamwork conception of the industrial enterprise which is generally more prevalent among supervisory and salaried staff than it is among hourly-paid operatives. It was hoped, too, that the involvement discussions and the consequent very real extension of plant democracy together with the transfer of responsibility for inspection from the supervisors, would all contribute to the emergence of more 'responsible' attitudes, in the sense that operatives would not only take on more responsibility for their day-to-day jobs, but would also identify themselves more strongly with the firm. In short, again there was the expectation that there would be less of the 'them and us' attitude, less of the perception of industry as two sides in conflict, and a strengthening of the unitary or teamwork concept.

As we saw in Chapter 1, other studies have shown that operatives may willingly accept the teamwork conception 'on the job', while at the same time, defining the situation as one of conflict when it comes to pay, believing that they could be paid more, and even believing their present pay to be inequitable. There is nothing contradictory about accepting the long-term coincidence of interest between management and men, and at the same time believing that the present bargain is unfair, in the sense that the 'cake' has not be fairly divided. There may be an awareness of areas in which there is substantial congruence of interest, for example, in the value of teamwork and co-operation on the job, and in the long-term economic viability of the firm. But side by side with this, there may be a consciousness of a conflict of interest over the actual division of the 'cake'.

We would not, then, expect this particular agreement necessarily to weaken a tough attitude towards the effort bargain. Indeed, as we saw in Chapter 4, although most operatives believed that they had benefited from the agreement, more than half thought that the Company had got the best of the bargain. Moreover, most, as we saw, went into the agreement for the money. Although some measure of increased job satisfaction was a spin-off, for most, money remains of major importance.

In short, labelling operatives 'salaried' is not likely to have much impact on attitudes. The situation *has* changed. Operatives do have much more say in job descriptions, more autonomy and responsibility. There *is* better teamwork and co-operation on the job. But their share of the 'cake' continues to be determined by tough collective bargaining. Although we have no direct evidence, other studies have shown that most operatives accept the view that in the long term, their interests and those of the firm coincide, in the sense that both have an interest in an efficient and profitable plant. In this plant there is generally a willingness to co-operate fully with management, a flexible attitude towards change, good teamwork and co-operation on the shop floor. But pay remains a matter for collective bargaining. And in some sections, a large proportion feel that the Company has had the best of the bargain.

We are not saying they are right. Indeed, as we pointed out in Chapter 4, there are surprising and marked differences between sections, which appear to be a reflection of more generalized feelings of contentment or deprivation with the context of the job. While the job remains essentially boring, noisy and unpleasant, money will continue to be seen as compensation. It is in such situations that feelings over money are most likely to run high, and a tough attitude towards the effort-bargain will persist.

Indeed, we cannot expect much from a change of 'status' from hourly paid to salaried. Collective bargaining remains the method for most by which increases in pay can be achieved. And this means trade unions and a union attitude towards pay in which the best effort-bargain is struck, with both sides trading, so far as they can, to their mutual advantage. In some occupations, advancement is by climbing a hierarchy of positions, each carrying high pay and status, in return for merit. This is not the future which faces the factory operative. It is this which is the crucial distinction between a career and a job. It is those who believe promotion is available as the reward for individual effort and achievement who do not join unions (though they frequently join some kind of protective association). For the man on the shop floor, his reward is still the effort-bargain struck by collective agreement. And for an increasing proportion of salaried workers whose chances of promotion in pay and status from effort are limited, there is an increased unionization and militancy reflecting the growing disenchantment with 'professionalism' and status as strategies for achieving 'equitable' pay.

Some changes in the formal industrial relations machinery have already been noted in Chapter 3 with the integration of the union machinery with the Works Council consultative structure. The new consultative/negotiating machinery had transformed the roles of line management and the personnel departments. Line management was now increasingly dealing with its own industrial relations issues resulting in a marked decrease in the involvement of the personnel manager who, eighteen months after the introduction of the agreement, stated that he had not been involved in a single negotiation since the new machinery.

What is much more problematic is the long-term impact of the changes on the 'balance of power' between management and men. Operatives have certainly gained greater influence over decisions which affect their day-to-day working. We can only raise the question whether this increase in industrial democracy and the drive towards a more unitary relationship will strengthen or weaken the influence of the unions in the formal negotiating machinery.

A successful agreement

Not all attempts at achieving similar productivity bargains have achieved the same degrees of success. Any diagnosis of the factors related to success or failure would take us beyond the confines of this study. It would require the long-term monitoring of a number of negotiations in different plants. We can only hazard a few informed guesses to account for the particular success (at least in the short run) of this agreement.

Firstly, there is no doubt about the commitment of senior management. Much is due to the drive and leadership of those who instigated the agreement and set going the series of discussions which preceded it. Although not all were convinced, they were willing to give it a try. There is little doubt too that the emphasis on involvement and shop-floor discussions from the outset were an essential ingredient. From the start, there was no suggestion that management had a blueprint. The stress was on participation, not negotiation and bargaining—on full involvement in thrashing out the best possible way to run the process. In short, in the words of a senior manager, 'there has been a major attempt to change the "culture" of the factory'.

But there were other important background factors. In 1966, there had been a major lay-off, making two hundred men redundant. This event had underlined the message that the plant could only survive by becoming more efficient. It is sited in a non-development area, and jobs depend heavily on its continued viability. Moreover, when the exercise had begun, the plant had been running at only 70 per cent of capacity, but this had risen to 100 per cent when the agreement was introduced. In short, the negotiations took place during a period of expanding demand.

Some measure of worker-involvement was not new. There had been a long tradition of putting the shop floor in the picture. For the preceding six years there had been an annual meeting at which senior management had talked to all levels of staff about the general financial position of the plant and its prospects. This had arisen partly out of the need in the early days to generate new attitudes towards costs and efficiency in the staff who were being recruited from the less competitive aircraft industry. Moreover, management had always attached importance to having highly trained supervisors, who were exposed to a substantial programme of in-service training. With a relatively stable labour force, many of whom had been with the plant since the start, this had made it possible to build up an atmosphere of trust and understanding. The stability of the labour force in turn is due in part to the geographical location of the plant, and the absence of comparable employment on any scale in the district. Many, especially the ex-miners, consider this the best job they've ever had, and want to see it continuing.

A further background factor of some importance in the initial acceptance of the decision to use this plant as a trial site was the government incomes policy. The full-time union officers had made it clear that it was only on the basis of a productivity agreement that increases could be negotiated.

As we have seen, those who stood to gain least, and even possibly to lose, were the craftsmen and the supervisors. The craft element in the plant is, in fact, relatively small. On a typical shift of four hundred, there are only about five craftsmen, and these tend to identify with the shift and to think of themselves as part of the team. Craft jobs had been changing slowly over the years and many of the less skilled jobs had already been given up. Even so, they were harder to win over. As one craftsman (quoted earlier) said, 'There'll be no apprenticeships . . . less skill will be required. You'll give a particular job away in stages'. Craft unions protect their members by delineating those jobs which can only be done by those who are licensed by holding a craft ticket (as do teachers, solicitors, doctors, and a whole range of occupations whose strength lies in the strategies they weave around expertise). The increased flexibility which was an essential element in the agreement is understandably seen by the craft unions as an erosion of their bargaining strength and the surrendering of the results of years of struggle. As previous studies have shown,[5] such attitudes and beliefs are deeply rooted in both history and experience. And 'the more notional the skill gap becomes, the greater the significance of the demarcation practices to the craftsmen. The fences are then more like a sea wall which stands between the inhabitants of the island and total flood.'[6]

However, at this site, there was no major opposition from the craftsmen. Nevertheless, agreements of this kind to decrease demarcation and increase flexibility can run into difficulties. Indeed, one possible source of difficulty is in the relations between craftsmen and their mates.[7] We did not find any significant evidence of this. There was one case which we quote, although we would stress that this example was not typical:

> 'It's increased the demarcation with the mates. They started getting cocky and refusing to do the jobs for us that they'd done as mates—they thought it was below them. So we put our foot down and drew rigid lines saying you can't do that because it's not in your write-up. . . . Instead of sending a craftsman and a mate to do a job they started sending two mates, but we soon put a stop to that. There's not much of our job we could give to operatives.'

Similarly, the supervisors too were well aware of the impact which the agreement would have on their traditional role. Not all felt able to adjust. And some found the transition a source of great strain. That the supervisors were, in general, won over, in some cases to enthusiastic support for the scheme, owes much to management skill.

---

[5] See, for example, A. Flanders, *op. cit.* (1964), pp. 214–16.

[6] *Ibid.*, p. 216.

[7] For a more extended discussion of the problems involved in the relations between craftsmen and mates, particularly over flexibility, see A. Flanders, *ibid.* (1964), pp. 166–82.

The Future

So, the agreement was by a number of criteria a success. Wages have increased, productivity has risen, quality has been maintained, greater flexibility has reduced boredom, there has been some increase in interest through job enlargement, and attitudes towards further change are generally favourable. Will it last? Will the memory of the real improvement fade into the background? Will the new present come to be taken for granted with a growing realization that the job is basically monotonous? We can only guess. There are strong grounds for arguing that some gains at least are permanent—the increased flexibility and a job which is far less boring. Perhaps the future is best summed up in the perceptive words of a spinning operative:

'I'd like to see it progressing indefinitely . . . you've probably absorbed enough to keep you going and interested for some time, but sooner or later the job's going to get boring again . . . I don't think we're ever going to come to a stage where we can sit still and say, "right, well, this is it . . . we're here". There's got to be another stage.'

In broad terms, one of the aims of this productivity agreement was to take a step in the direction of substituting an expressive for an instrumental orientation to work; to inject a greater interest into the job itself, with the aim of making work more satisfying and at the same time improving performance. Within the limits set by the technology, the exercise can be judged to have done much that it set out to do. But these limits are real. The relations between men and machines are substantially determined by the machines themselves, and therefore, in the last analysis, by those who design and make the machines. It is here, on the evolution of a more humane technology, that we must focus if we are to make real progress towards work which is meaningful and satisfying. Ergonomics is not enough. It is not effort, mere physical fatigue, which is the problem. Machines offer man the hope of emancipation from the drudgery of labour. But there is little ennobling about the assembly-line. However real the gains from greater insights

143

into man-management, it is the men who make the machines in whose hands the real powers for change are to be found.

There is a second limitation in the area of industrial relations. The gains in teamwork and co-operation resulting from increased participation were real. There is a genuine sense of teamwork on the shop floor and between management and men. But this does not extend to any radical change when it comes to pay and the effort-bargain. On this, there are still two sides facing each other over a table in collective bargaining. And in the short run, there is no necessary identity of interest. Such conflict is not necessarily damaging. The challenge here is to those responsible for its management and resolution.

Appendix

Methods of the Inquiry

The sample of sixty operatives was designed so that approximately equal proportions were drawn randomly from each of the three main areas of the shop floor and from each shift. It was decided to concentrate on the intensive interviewing of a relatively small sample. This method, it was felt, was likely to be the most effective way of achieving the objective of the inquiry, which was to obtain the fullest possible picture of the shop-floor feelings and reactions to the change.

In order to maximize rapport, a focused interview technique was used. The first step was to conduct a number of informal relatively unstructured interviews. During this preliminary period, a list of more specific questions was drawn up and constantly reviewed and revised. Before the main series of interviews, the precise questions to be put were memorized, and asked in the order which emerged as appropriate for each interview. In other words, the interviewee was given a fairly free rein to bring up those aspects of the work environment that he felt most strongly about, his comments and replies giving rise to further questions from the interviewer. The ideal aimed at was to make the subject aware of the objects of the research and to allow him to comment freely with the questions and answers following as naturally as possible. A small transistorized tape recorder was used to record the interviews. This was used with some hesitation at first even though each respondent was told that it was optional, would be heard only by the interviewer, and would be erased after coding. In the event, nobody demurred and its presence was quickly forgotten as the interview got under way. Although it made coding a lengthier process than it might otherwise have been, this method provided a complete and fully accurate account of the interview. It also allowed the interviews to flow smoothly from one subject to the next without interruption while lengthy responses were taken down, and the interviewer was able to devote all his attention to questioning and probing where necessary. The quality of the quotations in the text testify to the success of the interviews. Finally, although everyone was informed that participation was voluntary, the response rate was 100 per cent.

One point that should be kept in mind is that retrospective questions were included. This was unfortunately necessary because both time and resources were limited. Retrospective replies can never be entirely satisfactory as a basis for drawing conclusions and making inferences. But under the circumstances a reasonable compromise was arrived at. The agreement had been implemented ten weeks before the interviews began which was a long enough period of time for the impact of the bulk of the changes to have been felt by the operators. It was a time when they were probably most sensitive to the changes even though the process of change was still under way. But the pre-change period was sufficiently recent to permit reasonably accurate recall. Some of the interviews, however, notably of the supervisors and craftsman, were carried out some nine months after the agreement had been implemented.

Representativeness of the Sample and Statistical Significance

Whenever a sample is used in social research the question inevitably arises as to the applicability of the results to the population from which it is drawn. Of course, results based on a sample involve incomplete information about the population and therefore cannot be accepted as exact reflections of what we would find if the whole population were researched. And so we have to be content with a certain level of accuracy founded on probability. This level of accuracy depends on the way the sample is chosen, on sample size, and the variability of the findings.

If a sample is to represent a total population, then there must be no bias in its selection. Volunteers, for example, might be the most disgruntled, or the most enthusiastic. In other words, each member of the population must have the same chance of being chosen as any other. To ensure this, those we wished to interview were randomly selected from a complete list of operatives, so that each shift and each section was represented. The extent to which the sample reflects the population also depends on the proportion of the total included in the sample. In our case, the sampling fraction was approximately 4 per cent of the population.

The statistical significance of differences depends partly on the size of the differences and partly on the numbers in the sample. We wanted to be reasonably certain that any differences between, for example, the situation before the agreement and after it could not have occurred simply by chance. The smaller the numbers in the sample, the less confident we can be that any difference is meaningful. But the bigger the difference, the more confident we can be that it is significant. These two factors are taken care of by the statistical formulae. To give an example, if we find that 60 per cent of the sample reply 'yes' to a question, then there is only one chance in twenty that the actual percentage of the population replying 'yes' will be outside the limits 72·6 per cent and 47·4 per cent. In general, the differences discussed in this report are at least within these limits; that is, we have worked on a 0·05 (5 per cent) level of probability as the minimum. In Table 2.3, for example the probability is, in fact, less than 1:100 that this difference could occur by chance.

Index

For Product Safety Concerns and Information please contact our EU
representative GPSR@taylorandfrancis.com Taylor & Francis Verlag GmbH,
Kaufingerstraße 24, 80331 München, Germany

Printed and bound by CPI Group (UK) Ltd, Croydon, CR0 4YY
08/05/2025
01864380-0008